Mike McGrath

Linux

7th Edition

Illustrated using Linux Mint

In easy steps is an imprint of In Easy Steps Limited
16 Hamilton Terrace · Holly Walk · Leamington Spa
Warwickshire · United Kingdom · CV32 4LY
www.ineasysteps.com

Seventh Edition

Notice of Liability
Every effort has been made to ensure that this book contains accurate
and current information. However, In Easy Steps Limited and the
author shall not be liable for any loss or damage suffered by readers
as a result of any information contained herein.

Trademarks
All trademarks are acknowledged as belonging to their respective
companies.

In Easy Steps Limited supports The Forest Stewardship Council (FSC),
the leading international forest certification organization. All our titles
that are printed on Greenpeace approved FSC certified paper carry the
FSC logo.

MIX
Paper from
responsible sources
FSC® C020837

Printed and bound in the United Kingdom

ISBN 978-1-84078-937-9

Contents

Guess what? Wheels have been round for a really long time, and anybody who "reinvents" the new wheel is generally considered a crackpot. It turns out that "round" is simply a good form for a wheel to have. It may be boring, but it just tends to roll better than a square, and "hipness" has nothing what-so-ever to do with it.

Linus Torvalds, creator of the Linux kernel

1 Getting Started

Introducing Linux

Linux is a computer operating system that can run on a variety of hardware including the popular Intel system found on most desktop computers. It is a modern derivation of the powerful Unix operating system that was introduced way back in 1969. In recent years, the popularity of Linux has increased dramatically as computer users have discovered its many benefits:

Hot tip

Pronounce the name Linux with a short "i" – so it's "li-nucks", not "lie-nucks".

Don't forget

Many web servers are said to have a "LAMP" configuration – an acronym for **L**inux, **A**pache, **M**ySQL, **P**HP, which combines operating system, web server, database, and server-side scripting.

- Linux is released under the GNU Public License that ensures it can remain free to all users. It's available as a free download on the internet, but you may have to pay a distribution charge if you prefer a copy on CD/DVD.

- Access to the source code of Linux is unrestricted and it may be changed. This has allowed thousands of programmers around the world to refine the code to improve performance.

- Linux is truly a multi-user, multi-tasking operating system that allows multiple users to simultaneously work with multiple applications without experiencing any traffic problems. Many of the world's web servers run on Linux for this very reason.

- Linux is an extremely stable operating system – continuous uptimes of more than a year are not uncommon. It can be upgraded on the "fly" so it seldom needs a reboot.

- There are a large number of quality applications available to run on the Linux platform. These are comparable to commercial applications that run on other operating systems but, like Linux, these too are free of charge. For instance, the free LibreOffice suite offers similar functionality to the commercial Microsoft Office suite.

- With open-source software, an administrator can know exactly what a program can do and the security dangers it presents. An open-source application cannot secretly gather information about the user or send confidential information to third parties.

The Evolution of Linux

In 1983, a visionary programmer named Richard Stallman began a movement called the GNU Project. Its philosophy was that software should be free from restrictions against copying or modification in order to make better and more efficient programs. This inspired programmers around the world to create programs driven by efficiency rather than by financial incentive.

By 1991, the GNU Project had created a lot of software tools including the GNU C Compiler written by Stallman himself. At that time many of these tools were incorporated into a Unix-compatible operating system by a 21-year old student at the University of Helsinki. His name was Linus Torvalds and he named the operating system Linux (**Linu**s – Uni**x**).

Linux was made available for download on the internet so other programmers could test and tweak the source code, then return it to Linus Torvalds. After a period of enthusiastic development, Linux 1.0 was made available globally under the GNU General Public License, which ensured it would remain free.

Programmers were keen to explore Linux and soon found some amazing uses for it. In April 1996, researchers at Los Alamos National Laboratory used Linux to run 68 PCs as a single parallel processing machine to simulate atomic shock waves. At $150,000 this supercomputer cost just one-tenth the price of a comparable commercial machine. It reached a peak speed of 19 billion calculations per second, making it the 315th most powerful supercomputer in the world. It proved to be robust too – three months later it still didn't have to be rebooted.

Linux continued to grow in popularity as a text-based operating system, while Windows became the dominant graphical desktop operating system. Recognizing that most PC users want the point-and-click convenience of a graphical environment, the Linux camp began to develop a system comparable to the Windows desktop.

From a handful of enthusiasts in 1991 to millions of users now – Linux has come of age. Today's sleek K Desktop Environment (KDE) and the Gnome desktop environment now offer a user-friendly alternative for Windows users – Linux for the desktop!

This penguin is "Tux" – the happy Linux mascot.

The term "GNU" is a recursive acronym for **G**NU's **N**ot **U**nix. Discover more about the GNU General Public License online at gnu.org/licenses/gpl.html

Discover more about the Gnome graphical desktop online at gnome.org

Choosing a Distro

At the very heart of Linux is a bunch of tried-and-tested compiled code called the "kernel". The kernel provides the operating system with its core functionality, much like the engine in a car. It takes care of the basics, such as helping other programs access hardware and sharing your computer's processor among various programs.

In addition to the kernel, Linux contains a number of system-level programs, such as the services to handle your email, web connection and bootloader. Consider these as a car's transmission, gears, and chassis – without these, the engine is not much use.

Linux distributions generally also include a large number of user-level programs – the applications for daily use: for instance, web browsers, word processors, text editors, graphics editors, media players, and so on. These are the finishing touches to the car that ensure a great ride – whitewall tires and soft leather upholstery.

All of these components are bundled together in a wide variety of Linux distribution packages, commonly referred to as "distros" – just as all the components of a car are bundled together to make a complete car.

Most Linux distros are available as a "live" version that lets you run Linux from a disk – so you can try it out without installing Linux onto your hard drive.

In the same way that there are many makes and models of cars, there are many Linux distros to choose from. Some of the best known distros are RedHat Fedora, SUSE, Ubuntu, and Mint. Each distro has its own installer and unique default configuration according to what the distributor considers to be the best arrangement. The ideal one for you will depend on your own personal preferences and how you want to use Linux. The most popular distros are described below to help you choose:

RedHat Fedora

One of the most publicized Linux distros, comprising the commercial RedHat Enterprise Linux product line and the free Fedora distro that is developed by the Fedora Project community. There are several editions of the Fedora distro – "Workstation" for PCs, "Server" for servers, and "IoT" for cloud-based ecosystems.
Pros: Widely used, excellent community support, innovative.
Cons: Limited product life-span of Fedora editions, poor multimedia support.
Free download from **getfedora.org**

"Choose Freedom.
Choose Fedora."

openSUSE

The community-based "openSUSE" distro has received positive reviews for its installer and YaST configuration tools. The documentation, which comes with the boxed product, has been labeled as the most complete by far. The fixed release "Leap" distro is the base for the openSUSE award-winning SUSE Linux Enterprise (SLE) products, and the rolling release "Tumbleweed" distro provides the very latest stable versions of all software.

Pros: Attention to detail, easy-to-use YaST configuration tools.
Cons: Huge distro – including over 1,500 bundled packages.
Free download from **opensuse.org**

"The makers' choice for sysadmins, developers and desktop users."

Ubuntu

This sophisticated community distro typically employs the popular Gnome GUI desktop manager. It has the advantage of a fixed six-month release cycle, and every two years there is an LTS (**L**ong **T**erm **S**upport) release that is supported for five years. There are several editions of the Ubuntu distro – "Desktop" for PCs, "Server" for servers, "IoT" for Internet of Things devices, and "Cloud" for cloud computing. The default interface of the Ubuntu Desktop edition is quite different to that of the Windows desktop.

Pros: Great community, and fixed release cycle.
Cons: The interface will seem unfamiliar to Windows users.
Free download from **ubuntu.com**

"Fast, secure and simple, Ubuntu powers millions of PCs worldwide."

Linux Mint

A modern, elegant operating system that is easy to use. It is based on the Ubuntu operating system and works straight out of the box, with full multimedia support. All Linux Mint distros are LTS releases that appear shortly after each Ubuntu LTS release, and are supported for five years. Users are encouraged to send feedback so their ideas can be used to improve Linux Mint. This operating system typically employs the Cinnamon GUI desktop manager, which will feel familiar to those moving from the Windows operating system. For that reason, Mint is used throughout this book to demonstrate the features of a Linux operating system.

Pros: Great community, and the interface will seem familiar to Windows users – the best distro for beginners.
Cons: Ubuntu has a larger community of users than Mint.
Free download from **linuxmint.com**

"Linux Mint. From freedom came elegance".

Providing Disk Space

An operating system is installed on an area of the hard disk drive called a "partition". When Windows is the only installed operating system, its partition will normally occupy the entire hard drive. To install Linux in this situation there are three possible options:

A **H**ard **D**isk **D**rive (HDD or simply "hard drive") can be partitioned into one or more regions so that the operating system can manage each region separately.

- **Delete the Windows partition** – replacing it with Linux partitions that occupy the entire drive. This option will delete the Windows operating system along with all the applications and data files. It creates a dedicated Linux computer that will immediately start Linux when the PC gets switched on.

- **Reduce the Windows partition size** – so that it no longer occupies the entire drive, then create Linux partitions in the resulting free space. This option will retain the Windows operating system, applications and data files. It creates a "dual-boot" computer that allows the user to choose whether to start Linux or Windows whenever the PC gets switched on.

- **Add a second hard drive to the system** – this allows Linux partitions to occupy the entire second drive and retains the Windows operating system, applications and data files on the first drive. It too creates a dual-boot computer that allows the user to choose whether to start Linux or Windows whenever the PC gets switched on.

The option to install an additional hard drive for Linux is a popular choice for many people as they have often upgraded their original hard drive to a larger one, and so have their original drive spare. It also has several benefits over the other options:

Resizing partitions is a scary process where data loss can, and does, occur – even in expert hands. All contents of the partition must be backed up before attempting this operation.

- The free space on the Windows drive is not reduced.

- It removes the risk of data loss through partition resizing.

- The familiar Windows operating system is retained.

- It distinctly separates the two operating systems.

- Drive failure would only disrupt one operating system.

...cont'd

Adding a Second Hard Drive

Older IDE (Integrated Drive Electronics) hard drives need to be configured as a master/slave relationship by setting "jumpers" on the hard drive. The drives can then be connected in tandem by a single ribbon cable.

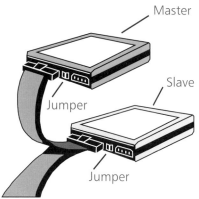

Master

Slave

Jumper

Jumper

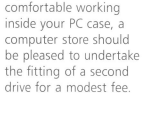

Hot tip

If you are not comfortable working inside your PC case, a computer store should be pleased to undertake the fitting of a second drive for a modest fee.

Most modern PCs now have SATA hard drives that do not need a master/slave configuration. Providing you have a Windows drive installed, your PC will automatically recognize an additional drive as secondary:

1. Turn off your PC, open up the case and find the existing hard drive – located in a cage

2. Install an additional SATA drive in the cage, then follow the cable of the first drive to identify where it plugs into the motherboard – usually a connector marked "SATA"

3. Plug your new drive's SATA cable into an adjacent SATA connector on the motherboard, and plug the other end into the new SATA drive itself

4. Attach a power cable from the PC's power unit to the SATA drive, then close the case and turn on your PC

5. Right-click the Start button and choose **Disk Management** to see an "Initialize Disk" dialog appear

6. Click **OK** to initialize the new hard drive, then back in Disk Management, right-click on the new drive and choose **New Simple Volume** from the context menu

7. Repeatedly click **Next** in the "New Simple Volume Wizard" to format the drive and allocate it a drive letter

SATA (**S**erial **A**dvanced **T**echnology **A**ttachment) is the standard for connecting devices to the PC's motherboard.

13

Creating Boot Media

The Linux Mint distro is available in three editions, with desktop environments called "Cinnamon", "MATE", and "Xfce" respectively. The most popular version is the Cinnamon edition that will be used throughout this book. It can be downloaded onto a USB flash drive to create "boot media". This lets you try out Linux without making changes to your system, and lets you install Linux onto your system if desired. But first you will need to ensure your system meets these minimum requirements:

- **1GB of RAM** (2GB preferred)

- **15GB of disk space** (20GB preferred)

- **1024 x 768 screen resolution**

Like other Linux distros, the Linux Mint download is an ISO image file whose content must be "burnt" onto the USB flash drive (not merely copied onto it) to create the boot media:

Hot tip

USB Flash Drive – also variously known as Thumb Drive, Pen Drive, Disk Key, Gig Stick, or Memory Stick.

1. Launch a web browser, then navigate to the download page **linuxmint.com/download.php**

2. Next, click on the **Cinnamon** link

Download links

EDITION	
Cinnamon	An edition featuring the Cinnamon desktop
MATE	An edition featuring the MATE desktop
Xfce	An edition featuring the Xfce desktop

3. Now, click a **Download mirror** link for your country from the list that appears

4. Choose to save the ISO image file in a preferred location on your system to begin the download

linuxmint.iso

5. When the download completes, you now need an app to burn the image onto the USB flash drive. Linux Mint recommends the **Etcher** app. Navigate your web browser to **balena.io/etcher** and download the installer for your system, such as "Download for Windows (x86/x64)"

6   When the installer download has completed, run its **Setup** wizard to install Etcher on your system

7   Next, connect a USB flash drive to your computer

8   Now, start the Etcher app and click the **Flash from file** button, then select the ISO image file you downloaded

If you wish to verify the ISO image file (recommended) you can find instructions on how to do so at **linuxmint-installation-guide. readthedocs.io/en/ latest/verify.html**

9   Click the **Select target** button, then select the USB flash drive you connected to your computer

10 Click the **Flash!** button to burn the contents of the ISO onto the USB flash drive – creating the Linux boot media

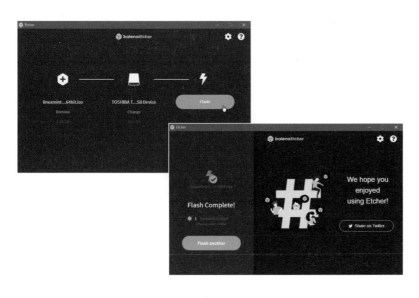

Starting a Live Session

Having created the boot media by following the steps on pages 14-15, you now have the ability to run Linux Mint in a "Live Session". This means you can safely explore the Linux operating system on a PC where Windows is already installed on the hard drive as its operating system.

In order to begin a Linux Live Session your PC must be able to boot up from the USB flash drive containing the boot media. This requires the PC's boot settings to seek instructions from the USB flash drive before seeking instructions on the hard drive. If your PC looks to boot from the hard drive first, you will need to change the settings:

Hot tip

The UEFI (**U**nified **E**xtensible **F**irmware **I**nterface) in modern PCs replaces the BIOS (**B**asic **I**nput/**O**utput **S**ystem) firmware interface in earlier PCs. These control how your PC boots up.

16

Don't forget

The Setup utility is unique to your PC, so its appearance will probably differ from the one shown here. Most PCs will, however, provide a way to change the Boot Priority Order so you can boot the PC from the USB flash drive.

1. Consult your PC's documentation to discover how to access its **Setup** utility. This often requires you to press the F2 key while starting the PC – but it does vary

2. Connect the USB flash drive boot media to your PC

3. Start up your PC and enter the Setup utility

4. Select the section relating to the PC's **Boot** process

Phoenix SecureCore Tiano Setup

| Information | Configuration | Security | **Boot** | Exit |

Item Specific Help

UEFI Boot   [Enabled]
Boot Priority Order

1. USB HDD: BOOT MEDIA
2. ATA HDD0:
3. ATA HDD1: ST9500423AS
4. ATAPI CD: MATSHITA DVD-RAM UJ8C1
5. USB FDD:
6. PCI LAN: Realtek PXE B03 D00
7. USB CD:

Use <↑> or <↓> select a device. Then press <F6> to move it up the list, or <F5> to move it down the list.

| F1 | Help | ↑↓ | Select Item | F5/F6 | Change Values | F9 | Setup Defaults |
| ESC | Exit | ←→ | Select Menu | Enter | Select ▶ Sub-Menu | F10 | Save and Exit |

---

5. Make the flash drive (USB HDD) the first boot device by following the Setup utility's **Help** instructions

6 Save the new settings and exit the Setup utility – typically by pressing the F10 key

7 If your PC is configured to boot in legacy BIOS mode, Linux Mint will now automatically start a Live Session

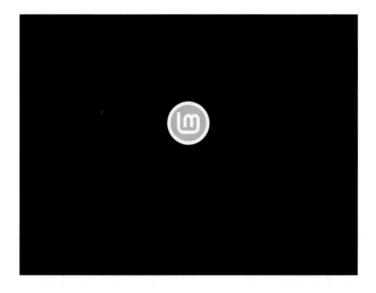

Hot tip

When there is an option to choose between UEFI boot mode and legacy BIOS mode, UEFI offers several advantages – UEFI supports large hard drive partitions, has secure booting, and provides efficient system management.

If your PC is configured to boot in UEFI mode, you will be presented with a menu. Select the "Start Linux Mint" option, then hit the **Enter** key to start a Live Session.

Welcome to Linux Mint 20.1 Cinnamon 64-bit

Start Linux Mint
Start in compatibility mode
OEM install (for manufacturers)
Integrity check
Hardware Detection
Boot from local drive
Memory test

Press [Tab] to edit options

Automatic boot in 8 seconds...

Hot tip

You may also see "UEFI" referred to as "EFI" – UEFI is simply EFI 2.0.

17

Beginning Installation

Having started a Live Session by following the steps on pages 16-17, you can try out the Linux Mint operating system. It will perform in a similar manner to when it is permanently installed on the hard drive, but with these notable exceptions:

● **The Live Session is slower** – it is loaded from the USB flash drive, rather than quickly from a hard drive.

● **Changes are not permanent** – they are not saved on the USB flash drive, or written anywhere on your PC.

● **Some apps behave differently** – system utilities, such as the Update Manager, cannot be used effectively.

The user name in a Live Session is "mint". If asked for a password you can simply hit the Enter key to proceed.

Live Session provides an installer icon on the Desktop that can be used to begin permanent installation of Linux Mint:

 Double-click on the "Install Linux Mint" icon to launch the Linux Mint installer wizard

...cont'd

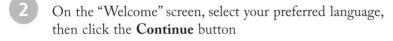

(2) On the "Welcome" screen, select your preferred language, then click the **Continue** button

This book features Linux Mint version 20 (Ulyssa) Cinnamon throughout. This version has Long Term Support until 2025.

(3) On the "Keyboard layout" screen, select your layout, then click the **Continue** button

If you are unsure of the keyboard layout you can type into this box and let the installer figure it out.

(4) Choose your wireless connection when asked, then check the box to install codecs and click the **Continue** button

Third-party codecs are required for multimedia support in certain apps. You are almost certainly going to want them.

Completing Installation

5 On the "Installation type" screen...

If you want only the Linux operating system on your PC (recommended), select **Erase disk and install Linux Mint**.

Or, if Windows is installed and you also want to keep that on your PC, select the option to **Install Linux Mint alongside Windows Boot Manager**.

If you retain Windows, the installer will resize the Windows operating system and install Linux in the free space created. A boot menu should appear so you can choose between operating systems whenever you start your PC – a "dual-boot" setup.

6 After choosing the installation type in either case, adjust the space suggested for each operating system if desired, then click the **Install Now** button to proceed

---

Hot tip

Advanced users can choose to manage disk partitions by choosing the **Something else** option here. Linux Mint requires one partition to be mounted on the root/directory. Although the operating system occupies around 15GB, this partition should ideally be 100GB+.

Beware

Attempting to create a dual-boot setup can be problematic on some PCs – erase the entire disk and install Linux Mint.

7 On the "Where are you?" screen, select your timezone then click the **Continue** button

Hot tip

Simply click your approximate location on the global map to select your timezone.

8 On the "Who are you?" screen, enter your details then click the **Continue** button to install system files

Hot tip

If you are the only user of the PC you can select the option to **Log in automatically** so you will not be asked for your password whenever you start Linux Mint. You may also select the **Encrypt my home folder** option if you are concerned about security.

21

9 Enjoy the slideshow while Linux Mint gets installed, then upon completion click the **Restart Now** button

Hot tip

For help with installation refer to the online Linux Mint forums at **forums.linuxmint.com**

Enabling Backups

Having completed the installation process by following the steps on pages 18-21, Linux Mint will launch to your Desktop. Before you start using the operating system it is recommended you enable the "Timeshift" backup utility. This is like "System Restore" on Windows and will allow you to restore the operating system to an earlier backup should any problems arise:

1 Click on **Menu** ("Start" button), **Administration**, **Timeshift**

2 Next, enter the password you chose in the "Who are you?" dialog during the installation process, then click the **Authenticate** button

3 Now, select the "RSYNC" option, then click the **Next** button

Hot tip

"RSYNC" is a disk-based backup system that only backs up what has changed since the previous backup.

4 Select the device on which you want the system backup snapshots to be saved, then click the **Next** button. (Here, the chosen device is an external hard drive that is connected, but you could alternatively connect a USB flash drive and choose that device for backups

Do not choose your main hard drive as the location at which to save backup snapshots – this would not help you if your hard drive fails.

5 Select the monthly, weekly, daily and hourly frequency for when you would like system backup snapshots to be saved on your chosen device, then click the **Finish** button

Backup snapshots are saved in a newly-created **timeshift** directory at the root level on the chosen device. Boot snapshots are performed in the background so do not affect the speed at which the system boots.

6 Re-open Timeshift in the future and select a saved backup snapshot, then click the **Restore** button to restore your Linux Mint system

23

Summary

- **Linux** is a free, stable multi-user operating system that is derived from the powerful Unix operating system.

- The name "Linux" combines letters from the first name of its originator, **Linu**s Torvalds, with the final letter of Uni**x**.

- Both **KDE** and the **Gnome** desktop are user-friendly graphical user interfaces, providing the same point-and-click convenience of the Windows desktop.

- The **kernel** provides the core functionality of Linux.

- Linux **distros** bundle the kernel, system-level programs, and free user-level programs in a variety of combinations.

- The most popular Linux Mint distro employs the **Cinnamon** desktop manager, and is the best distro for beginners.

- Minimum hardware **requirements** to run Linux Mint are 1GB of RAM, 15GB of disk space, and a screen resolution of 1024 x 768 – but higher specifications will perform better.

- A second **hard drive** can easily be added to a PC so it can dual-boot to Linux or Windows.

- A Linux distro can be downloaded and burned as a file system image onto a USB flash drive to create **boot media**.

- In order to boot from a USB flash drive it may be necessary to change the boot device order using the boot **Setup utility**.

- A **Live Session** lets you try out most features of Linux Mint before installation, and also provides an installer.

- The Linux Mint **installer** allows you to install Linux as the sole operating system, or install it alongside Windows.

- Before you start using the Linux Mint operating system it is recommended you enable the **Timeshift** backup utility so you can restore your system should problems arise.

2 Exploring the Desktop

Meeting the Interface

When you start up the Linux Mint operating system, the first thing you see while the system begins loading is a black screen displaying only the Linux Mint logo:

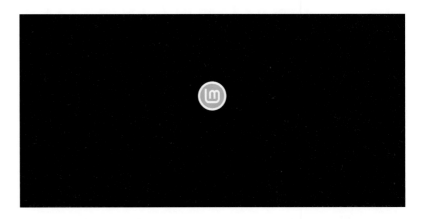

The distro featured throughout this book is Linux Mint 20 (Ulyssa).

Unless you selected the option to "Log in automatically" during the installation process (as described on page 21), the next thing you see is the **Log in** screen shown below:

The current time is also shown at the top right of the **Log in** screen. Hover your mouse cursor above the time to see the current date appear in a pop-up **Tooltip** box.

Computer Name   Username   Accessibility   Keyboard Layout   Quit

Password

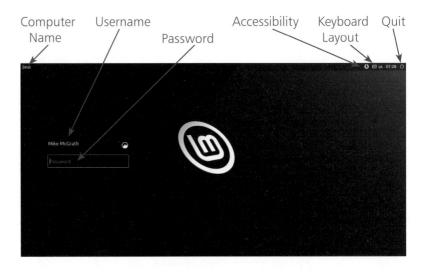

You can now enter the password you chose, then click the arrow button that appears in the password box (or hit the **Enter** key) to log in to the Linux Mint operating system.

After you log into Linux Mint, whether via the **Log in** screen or by choosing the automatic option, the GUI (**G**raphical **U**ser **I**nterface) Desktop and Taskbar will appear, as shown below:

Desktop Shortcuts   Desktop Wallpaper

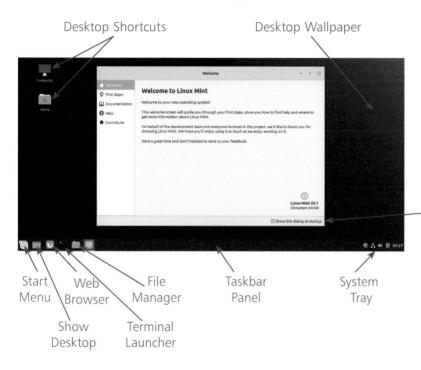

Start Menu

Web Browser

Show Desktop

Terminal Launcher

File Manager

Taskbar Panel

System Tray

The **Welcome** dialog provides helpful information for new users. Uncheck this option if you don't want to see this dialog again. Click the **X** button in the top right of any window to close that window.

27

If you have experience of the Windows operating system, the Linux Mint Desktop will seem familiar – as is the intention.

System Tray
The System Tray contains, by default, five icons that provide access to useful features when you click on the icon:

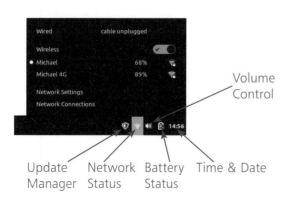

Update Manager

Network Status

Battery Status

Time & Date

Volume Control

Hover your mouse cursor above any System Tray icon to see information appear in a pop-up **Tooltip** box.

Configuring the Desktop

One of the first changes many people want to make to their Linux Desktop is to the background "wallpaper" of the Desktop:

1 Right-click anywhere on the Desktop wallpaper – to open a context menu

Create New Folder
Create New Document ▸
Add Desklets
Change Desktop Background
Create a new launcher here...
Open in Terminal
Open as Root
Customize
Paste

2 Select the **Change Desktop Background** option – to open a "Backgrounds" settings window

Hot tip

You can click the **Settings** button to adjust how the image fits your Desktop, or to choose a background color instead of an image.

3 Choose **Ulyssa** in the left-hand pane – to see a selection of wallpaper images appear in the right-hand pane

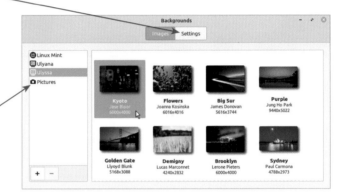

Hot tip

You can also click on the **Pictures** folder to choose one of your own images.

4 Scroll down and click on any image – to see it instantly applied as background wallpaper on your Desktop

...cont'd

If you are used to seeing the "Recycle Bin" icon on the Windows Desktop, or would simply like to restore deleted files easily, you will want to see the "Trash" icon on Linux Mint's Desktop:

1 Right-click anywhere on the Desktop wallpaper to open the context menu and select **Customize** – to open a "Current Monitor Layout" window

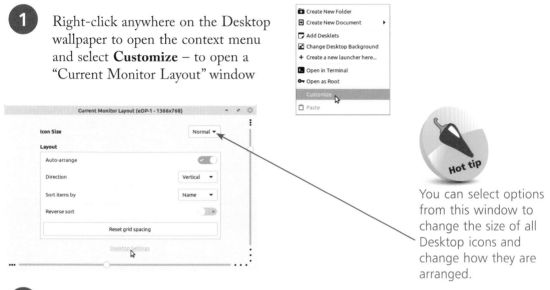

You can select options from this window to change the size of all Desktop icons and change how they are arranged.

2 Next, click the **Desktop Settings** link – to open a "Desktop" window

3 See that the toggle switch for the **Trash** icon is in the "Off" position

4 Slide the toggle switch to the "On" position to see the Trash icon now appear on the Desktop

Adding Desklets

Linux Mint offers a number of small apps ("applets") that run on the Desktop. These are similar to the Desktop widgets you may have seen in Windows, but are called "Desklets" (**Desk**top app**lets**) in Linux Mint. Some desklets are installed as standard, and you can download many more:

1 Right-click anywhere on the Desktop wallpaper to open the context menu, then select **Add Desklets** – to open a "Desklets" settings window

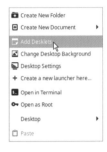

2 Next, select an installed desklet, such as the **Clock desklet**

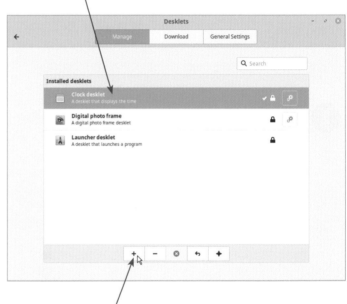

Hot tip

You can click the **General Settings** button in the Desklets window to modify width and decoration aspects of your desklets.

30

3 Now, click the **+ Add** button to instantly add the desklet to your Desktop

Don't forget

You can drag desklets around the Desktop to arrange them to your preference.

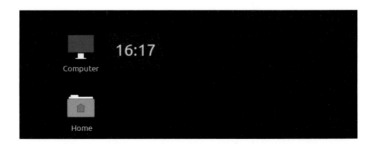

4 Click the **Download** button, then choose a desklet and click the Down arrow button to install it on your PC

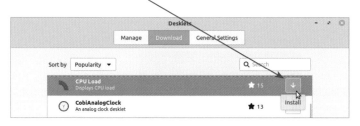

5 Click the **Manage** button to see your chosen desklet has been added to the list of installed desklets

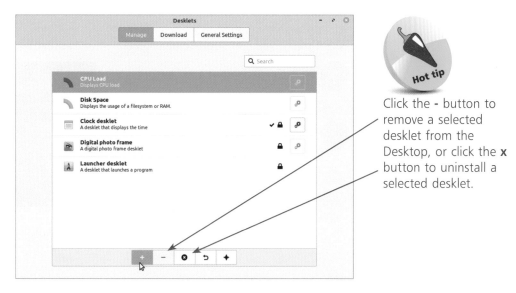

31

6 Select the newly-installed desklet, then click the **+ Add** button to instantly add it to your Desktop

Adjusting the Taskbar

The Taskbar panel contains an icon for each running app window that you can click to restore a minimized window to its original size. Usefully, you can hover the mouse cursor over the icon of a minimized app to see a thumbnail preview of that window:

Additionally, you can add useful applets to the Taskbar panel:

1 Right-click on the **Taskbar** to open a context menu

2 Select the **Applets** option – to open an "Applets" settings window

Hot tip
You can click the **Panel settings** item on this context menu for options to automatically hide the Taskbar panel, add more panels, and edit panels.

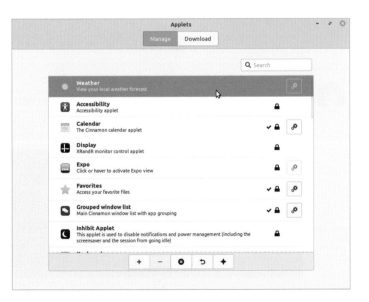

Hot tip
Notice that the **Applets** settings window functions much like the **Desklets** settings window described on page 30.

...cont'd

 3 Click the **Manage** button to select from a list of installed applets, or click the **Download** button to install another applet – for example, download the "Weather" applet

4 Click the **Manage** button and select the Weather applet, then click the **+ Add** button to add it to the Taskbar panel

 5 The weather app should detect your location, but also allows you to choose a location. Right-click on the applet then choose the **Configure** option

6 In the Weather settings window, click the **Location** button then slide the **Manual Location** button to "On"

7 Next, type a preferred city name into the **Location** box, then close the window

8 Now, click the Taskbar applet to see the weather for your chosen location

Hot tip

Right-click on an applet to see a context menu that offers configuration options and an option to remove the applet from the Desktop.

Launching Apps

Apps can be launched in Linux Mint from the (Start) Menu and additional launchers can easily be added to the Taskbar, or on the Desktop, for frequently-used applications:

1 Click the **Menu** button, at the far left of the Taskbar, then position the mouse pointer over the **Accessories** category to see that category's list of apps

2 On the Accessories menu list, click the **Text Editor** item to launch the Text Editor app

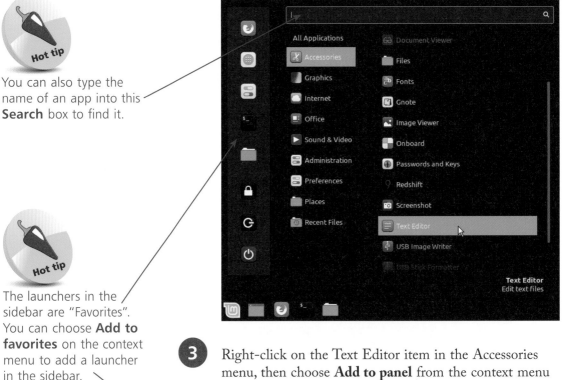

3 Right-click on the Text Editor item in the Accessories menu, then choose **Add to panel** from the context menu to create a launcher button on the Taskbar

4 Click the new launcher that has been added to the Taskbar to launch the Text Editor

5 Right-click on the Text Editor item in the Accessories menu, then choose **Add to desktop** from the context menu to create a launcher icon on the Desktop

6 Click the shortcut launcher icon that has been added to the Desktop, to launch the Text Editor

You can also create a Desktop launcher icon for any application if you know its precise command name. In this instance, the Text Editor for the Cinnamon Desktop is named "xed".

7 Right-click on the Desktop, then choose **Create a new launcher here** from the context menu that appears

8 Type a name and the **xed** command name into the appropriate input fields in the "Launcher Properties" dialog, then click its **OK** button to create the Desktop launcher

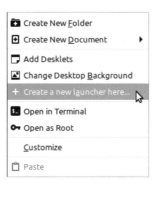

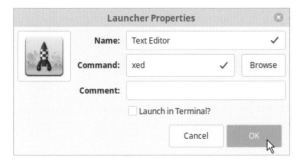

To delete a launcher from the Taskbar, right-click on it and choose **Remove**. To remove a launcher from the Desktop, right-click on it and choose **Delete**.

You can also launch apps from a command prompt in a Terminal window. Simply type the app's command (**xed** in this case) then hit the **Enter** key to launch the app.

35

Editing the Menu

Like many things in the Linux Mint operating system, the (Start) Menu can be customized to suit your personal taste:

 Right-click on the **Menu** button, at the far left of the Taskbar, then select the **Configure** option

 Click the **Panel** button and slide the **Use a custom icon and label** toggle button to "On"

 Select from options to adjust **Appearance** and **Behavior**. For example, change the Menu button's **Text** value

36

 See that your selected options are instantly applied to the Menu

 Click the **Menu** button in the "Menu" window, then click the **Open the menu editor** button

You can click the hamburger button and save your Menu settings as a file, which can be imported later to resume those settings.

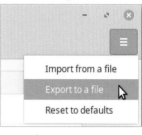

5 Slide all toggle switches to the "Off" position to simplify the Menu

6 Now, click the **Open the menu editor** button

7 Click any category in the left-hand pane, then select Menu items in the right-hand pane

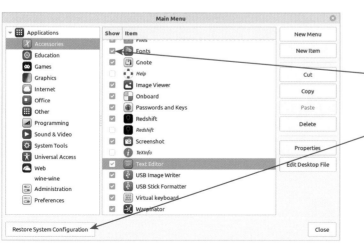

You can uncheck the individual items to remove them from the Menu and click the **Restore System Configuration** button to resume its default appearance.

37

Installing Updates

Having set up Timeshift to make regular backups of your Linux Mint operating system (see page 22), it is recommended that you regularly apply all updates available for your system:

 Connect your PC to the internet then click **Menu**, **Administration**, **Update Manager**, or click the 🛡 Update Manager icon on the system tray to open an "Update Manager" window

 If the Update Manager suggests you switch to a local mirror server, click this **Yes** button

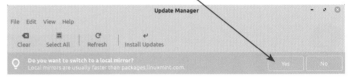

Hot tip

A "Welcome" screen may appear when you first open the Update Manager. Click its **OK** button to proceed.

3️⃣ Enter your password, then click the **Authenticate** button – to open a "Software Sources" dialog

4️⃣ Double-click in the **Main (ulyssa)** box and select a local mirror from the list that appears, then click **Apply**

 Now, select a local mirror for the **Base (focal)** box, then click **OK** to close the "Software Sources" dialog

6 Wait while the software list gets updated, then return to the "Update Manager" window

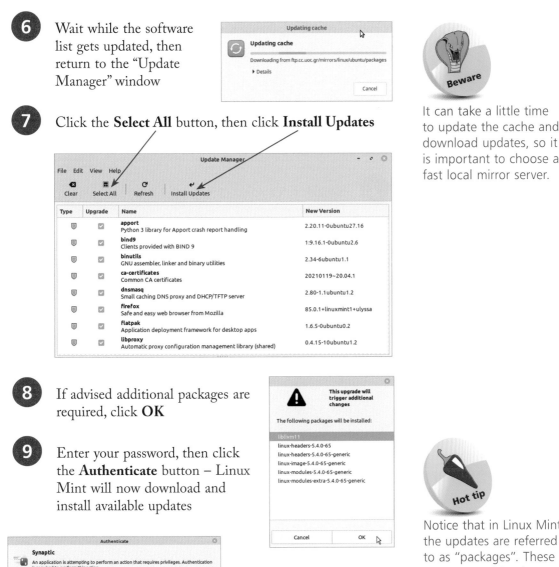

It can take a little time to update the cache and download updates, so it is important to choose a fast local mirror server.

7 Click the **Select All** button, then click **Install Updates**

8 If advised additional packages are required, click **OK**

9 Enter your password, then click the **Authenticate** button – Linux Mint will now download and install available updates

Notice that in Linux Mint the updates are referred to as "packages". These are managed by the **Synaptic Package Manager**, which can be found in the Administration category on the Menu.

Closing the Desktop

If your Linux Mint operating system is left unused it will, by default, automatically replace the Desktop with a screensaver and lock the screen. This means you will need to enter your password to get back to the Desktop. If you wish to leave your PC, you can immediately lock the screen for security purposes:

 Click the **Menu button**, then click the "Lock screen" button to instantly close the Desktop

2 See the screensaver now fills the screen so your PC cannot be used

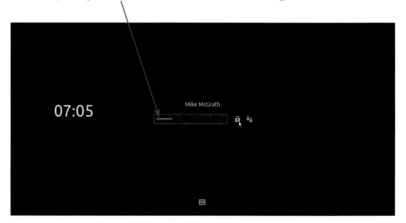

Hot tip

You can also lock the screen using the **Ctrl** + **Alt** + **L** keyboard shortcut. To discover more Linux Mint shortcuts, click **Menu**, **Preferences**, **Keyboard** to open the "Keyboard" window, then click the **Shortcuts** button. Select a category, such as **System**, in the left-hand pane to see available shortcuts in the right-hand pane.

40

 Move your mouse when you want to unlock your PC, and you will be presented with a password request – enter your password to return to the Desktop

Hot tip

You can click the ⏏ **Switch User** button to log out – you will then see the **Log in** screen illustrated on page 26.

You may sometimes want to log out of the Linux Mint operating system for security purposes or to switch users:

 Click **Menu**, then click the "Log Out" button to see a "Session" options dialog appear

 Click the **Log Out** option button, or the **Switch User** option button, to see the **Log in** screen appear

When you are going to be away from your PC for a long time you will probably want to shut down the operating system:

 Click **Menu**, then click the "Quit" button to see a "Shut down this system now?" options dialog appear

 Click the **Shut Down** option button to exit Linux Mint and power off your PC

Hot tip

The **Switch User** option saves your session state to allow someone else to log in. When they log out and you log back in, you will be back where you left off – your open apps will still be running. The **Log Out** option, on the other hand, ends the session and closes your open apps – when you log back in they will not be running.

Hot tip

The **Suspend** option stops all apps, and the system state is saved in RAM as your PC goes into low-power mode. Hit any key to awaken the PC exactly where you left off.

Summary

● Unless the "Log in automatically" option was selected during installation, the **Log in** screen will request your password whenever you start the Linux Mint operating system.

● The Linux Mint GUI comprises a **Desktop** and **Taskbar**.

● The **Desktop** contains shortcuts and background wallpaper.

● The **Taskbar** panel contains a Menu button, Show Desktop button, app launchers, and the System Tray.

● The **System Tray** gives access to Update Manager, Network Status, Battery Status, Time & Date, and Volume Control.

● The Desktop can be configured to have different background **Wallpaper** and to contain different **Shortcut** icons.

● **Desklets** are small apps that run on the Desktop.

● Hovering the mouse cursor over the Taskbar icon of a running app will display a **Thumbnail Preview** of that app.

● Useful **applets** can be added to the Taskbar panel.

● App launchers are grouped by **category** on the Menu.

● App launchers can be added to the **Taskbar** and **Desktop**.

● The Menu can be configured to customize its **Appearance** and its **Behavior**.

● With the Timeshift backup utility enabled, all updates can be regularly applied with the **Update Manager** app.

● Selecting local mirrors as **Software Sources** usually allows updates to be downloaded faster.

● The Desktop can be closed by switching to the **Lock screen** for security.

● The **Log Out** option and **Switch User** option closes the Desktop and opens the **Log in** screen.

● The **Shut Down** option closes the Desktop and powers off the PC.

3 Setting Preferences

This chapter describes some useful ways you can set up your Linux Mint system to suit your preferences.

Configuring the Screensaver

By default, your Linux Mint Desktop will automatically switch to the screensaver if you do not interact with your PC for a while. This means you may frequently have to enter your password to return to the Desktop and is unnecessary if your PC is located in an environment where security is not a concern. Fortunately, you can disable this behavior so the Desktop will always be visible unless you choose to explicitly lock the PC.

You may also choose how the screen appears by selecting a custom screensaver, and you can add a message to the Lock screen:

1 Click **Menu**, **Preferences**, **Screensaver** to open a "Screensaver" window

2 Next, click the **Settings** button

Hot tip

Notice that you can choose to extend the delay before the screensaver will appear if you don't want to totally disable the screensaver.

3 Now, open the drop-down menu for "Screensaver settings" and select the **Never** option – to stop your PC automatically switching to the Lock screen

4 Choose preferences from the **Lock settings** section

5 Next, click the **Customize** button

6 Type a custom **Away message** to be displayed on the Lock screen

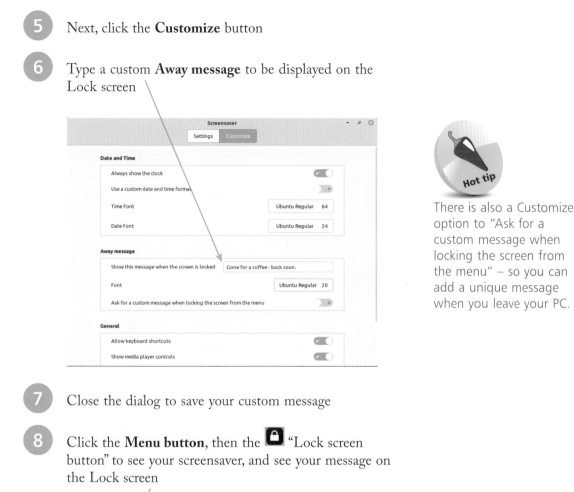

45

7 Close the dialog to save your custom message

8 Click the **Menu button**, then the "Lock screen button" to see your screensaver, and see your message on the Lock screen

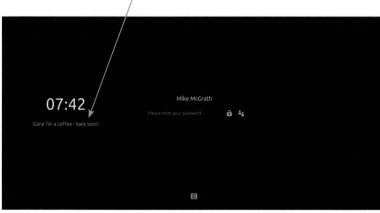

Managing Windows

The control buttons on the Linux Mint window title bars perform the same actions as those in the Windows operating system:

Minimize to Taskbar   Maximize/Reduce Size   Close Window

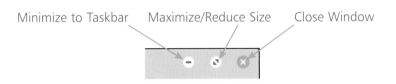

You can also snap windows to the screen edges, tile windows to the corners of the screen, and move windows between workspaces:

 Click **Menu**, **Accessories**, **Text Editor** to open the Text Editor app

 Click the window's control button to reduce it from full-screen size

 Next, click on the window's title bar and hold down the mouse button, then drag the window to any screen edge

When you see a zone preview, release the mouse button to snap the window to that edge – filling half of your screen

46

Hot tip

Windows that are not full-size snapped or tiled can be resized by dragging their edges or corners.

Hot tip

You can ignore the on-screen instruction to **Hold <Ctrl>**. Simply snap two apps to the left and right sides of your screen to work on two documents at the same time.

Now, click on the window's title bar and hold down the mouse button, then drag the window to any screen corner

6 When you see a zone preview, release the mouse button to snap the window to that corner – filling a quarter of your screen

Don't forget

You can tile up to four apps. Also, you can snap and tile. For example, tile two apps at the top corners and snap another app across the bottom half of the screen to work on three documents at the same time.

7 Click **Menu, Preferences, Hot Corners** to open a "Hot Corners" window

8 Enable the top left-hand corner to show workspaces, then move the mouse cursor to that corner to see the workspaces

Hot tip

You can drag apps from one workspace to another and click any workspace to begin working there in full screen. The apps remain running on the hidden workspaces so you can switch back to them.

Personalizing Options

You can personalize the behavior and appearance of windows by specifying preferences on your Linux Mint operating system. For example, many people prefer to change the default light gray windows to dark gray:

1 Click **Menu**, **Preferences**, **Window Tiling** to open a "Window Tiling" window – here you can disable Tiling and Snapping or modify its behavior

Hot tip

Slide this toggle switch to the "Off" position to disable the **Hold <Ctrl>** message when snapping or tiling your windows.

Window Tiling	− ⌀ ○
←	
Enable Window Tiling and Snapping	⬤
Tiling and Snapping	
Tiling HUD visibility threshold (Pixels)	25 − +
Modifier to use for toggling between tile and snap mode	Control ▼
Maximize, instead of tile, when dragging a window to the top edge	○✕
Show snap on-screen-display	⬤
Show tile heads-up-display	⬤
Legacy window snapping (hold <Shift> while dragging a window)	○✕

2 Click **Menu**, **Preferences**, **Windows** to open a "Windows" window – here you can modify title bar actions and window actions

Hot tip

Click the **Alt-Tab** button at the top of the dialog and explore switcher style options. To use the window switcher hold down the **Alt** key then jab the **Tab** key to select a window. Release the **Alt** key to give that window focus.

Windows	− ⌀ ○
Titlebar Behavior Alt-Tab	
Buttons	
Buttons layout	Right ▼
Actions	
Action on title bar double-click	Toggle Maximize ▼
Action on title bar middle-click	Lower ▼
Action on title bar right-click	Menu ▼
Action on title bar with mouse scroll	Nothing ▼

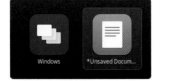

3 Click **Menu**, **Preferences**, **Themes** to open a "Themes" window, then click the **Themes** button to see the current appearance settings

48

...cont'd

Click the **Add/Remove** button to see a list of themes you can download and install. These provide additional options on the fly-out menu for the Desktop.

4   Click the current **Mint-Y** setting for "Window borders" to open a fly-out menu, then select the **Mint-Y-Dark** option to instantly change the border appearance

5   Similarly, click the current **Mint-Y** setting for "Controls", then select **Mint-Y-Dark** on the fly-out menu to instantly change the appearance of window controls

49

Click the **Settings** button to see options to show or hide icons on window buttons and menus.

Controlling Connections

Linux Mint allows you to easily control how you connect to the internet via wireless Wi-Fi or wired Ethernet connections. You can also mask your presence via a proxy server or through a Virtual Private Network (VPN) connection:

1 Click **Menu, Preferences, Network** to open a "Network" window, then click **Wi-Fi** in the left-hand pane – to see available wireless connections in the right-hand pane

Don't forget

You can also click the "Wireless connection" icon on the **System Tray** to view network status.

2 Similarly, click **Wired** to see available wired connections

3 Click **Network proxy** to see or add details for a proxy server with which you could mask your presence

Hot tip

Proxy servers and VPNs both hide your IP address but, unlike VPNs, proxies do not encrypt your connection – it is safer to use a VPN to mask your presence.

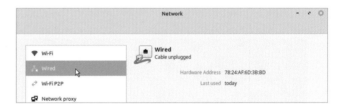

...cont'd

4 Click the + **Add** button to open an "Add VPN" dialog, then choose the **Point-to-Point Tunneling Protocol (PPTP)** option

5 Next, enter the Name, URL, and User details of your VPN service, then click the **Advanced** button

You will need to click this icon and choose whether to store the password before you can enter a password.

6 Select authentication and security options and click OK, then click the + **Add** button on the "Add VPN" dialog

7 Click the newly-added VPN entry in the "Network" window, then slide the toggle switch to the "On" position to connect

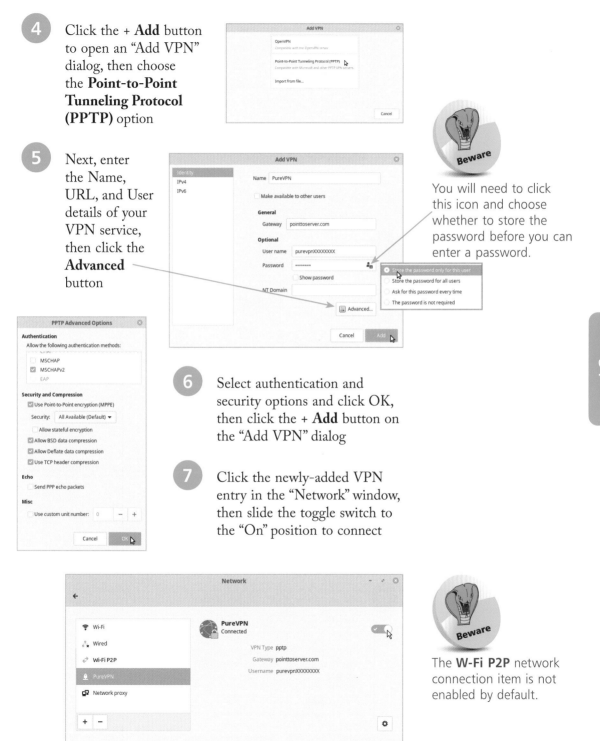

The **W-Fi P2P** network connection item is not enabled by default.

Adding Printers

Linux Mint provides drivers for a wide range of printers, so adding a printer is often simply a matter of connecting the printer to a USB port on your PC and turning the printer on. The operating system should recognize the printer and display a notification that it has been automatically added to your system:

The properties and options of added printers can be found in the "Printers" app, which can also be used to add network printers:

1 Click **Menu**, **Administration**, **Printers** to open a "Printers" window

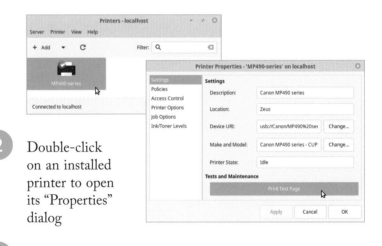

2 Double-click on an installed printer to open its "Properties" dialog

3 Next, turn on a network printer and press its Wi-Fi button to make it visible to the network

4 Now, click the + **Add** button on the "Printers" window – to open a "New Printers" dialog, listing available printers

You can click the **Print Test Page** button on the "Properties" dialog to test your printer.

Click the **Printer** menu and select the **View Print Queue** option to open a "Document Print Status" dialog where you can control print jobs.

5 Expand the **Network Printer** category, then select your printer and click the **Forward** button

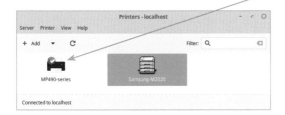

Hot tip

If your printer is not immediately listed you can click the **Find Network Printer** option to seek your printer.

6 Enter a name and description of the printer, then click the **Apply** button

Hot tip

The printer icon marked with a check mark denotes the system-wide default printer. You can change the default printer from its right-click context menu.

7 See that the network printer is now added to the "Printers" window and is ready to print

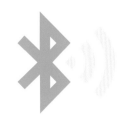

Pairing via Bluetooth

Linux Mint allows you to connect an external device that supports Bluetooth wireless technology, such as a wireless Bluetooth speaker, using a USB dongle and the Bluetooth device manager:

1 Connect a Bluetooth dongle to a USB port on your PC, or enable Bluetooth if it's already present on your system

You only need to connect a dongle if your PC does not have a built-in Bluetooth adapter.

2 Turn on the wireless Bluetooth speaker

54

3 Press and hold the speaker's "pairing" button to switch the speaker into pairing mode

4 On your PC, click **Menu**, **Preferences**, **Bluetooth** to open the Bluetooth device manager

Slide the toggle switch on the Bluetooth device manager to enable or disable Bluetooth.

5 To search for nearby Bluetooth devices, slide the toggle switch to the "On" position

6 When the speaker is found, click on the wireless speaker item in the "Devices" list to pair it with your PC

Hot tip

For security reasons the Bluetooth device manager may sometimes require you to confirm a device's PIN in order to establish a connection.

7 When the speaker is connected, the "Not Set Up" message changes to "Connected"

Beware

Once paired, you can disconnect and reconnect to the device, but if you remove it you will need to pair it again to re-establish a connection.

55

8 Click on the wireless speaker item in the "Devices" list to see its status dialog

9 Place the cursor over the Bluetooth icon that has been automatically added to the System Tray to see the connection details

Summary

- The **Screensaver** app can be used to disable the screensaver or to choose an animated screensaver.

- The **Lock screen** can be customized to display an "Away message" for times when the user is absent.

- The window title bars in Linux Mint contain familiar **Minimize**, **Maximize/Reduce**, and **Close** buttons.

- Windows can be **Snapped** to the screen edges and **Tiled** to the screen corners.

- The **Hot Corner** feature can be enabled to display workspaces.

- Windows can be dragged from one **Workspace** to another and the apps will remain running on hidden workspaces.

- The **Window Tiling** app can be used to disable Tiling and Snapping or to modify their behavior.

- The **Windows** app can be used to modify title bar actions and to modify window actions.

- A window can be selected with the **Window Switcher** feature by pressing the Alt and Tab keyboard keys.

- The **Themes** app can be used to change the look of Window Borders, Icons, Controls, Mouse Pointer, and Desktop.

- Wi-Fi connections, wired connections, and proxy connections can be controlled with the **Network** app.

- The Network app can also be used to add a **VPN** connection to mask your presence when online.

- Linux Mint should automatically detect and add a **Printer** when it is directly connected to the PC.

- The **Printers** app can be used to add a network printer to the system to enable printing via a Wi-Fi connection.

- The **Bluetooth** app can be used to pair the PC with a nearby Bluetooth device.

4 Touring the File System

Meeting the Directory Tree

When moving from Windows, the new Linux user needs to be aware of some differences between the two operating systems:

- Linux is case-sensitive – Windows is not. For instance, files named "readme.txt" and "README.txt" are seen as two different files in Linux, but there is no distinction in Windows.

- Linux directories and files have ownership permissions that can restrict accessibility to the owner or group – Windows directories and files are generally universally accessible.

- Linux was developed as a multi-user network operating system – Windows evolved from MS-DOS (**M**icro**s**oft **D**isk **O**perating **S**ystem) as a single-user home operating system.

- Linux desktop users cannot change system settings; only the "root" superuser may do so – Windows desktop users have free reign to wreak havoc.

- Linux partitions are created using the Ext4 file system – Windows partitions use FAT, FAT32 or NTFS file systems.

- Linux path names contain forward slash characters – Windows path names contain backslash characters: for instance, a Linux path **/home/mike** and a Windows path **C:\Users\mike**.

- Linux does not have any drive letters – Windows typically uses C: for the hard disk drive, D: for the optical drive, E: for an external drive, and so on.

The lack of drive letters in Linux indicates what is, probably, the biggest difference between Linux and Windows – the way their directory structures are arranged. In Linux, everything is contained within a single unified hierarchical system – beginning with the "root" directory, symbolized by a single forward slash "/".

The Linux installation creates a number of standard sub-directories within the root directory. Each one of these, in turn, houses its own sub-directory structure, thereby creating a directory "tree" – the "root" directory of / is the root of the tree.

See page 72 and page 174 for more on access permissions.

See page 170 for more on the Linux file system.

Contents of peripheral drives appear in the tree in the directory at which they are "mounted" by Linux, creating a unified structure. The table below lists the directory structure of the Linux Mint file system. All are sub-directories of the basic root directory "/".

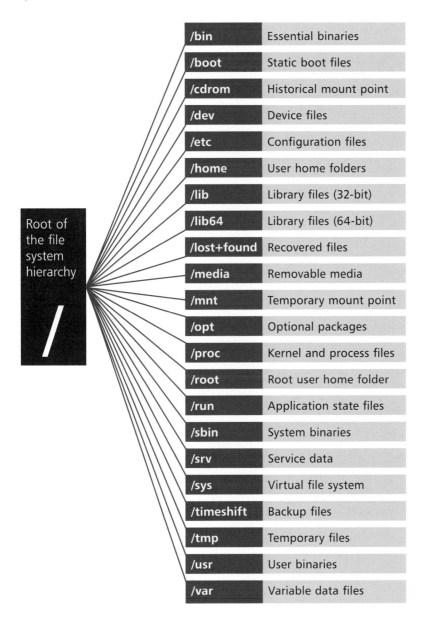

Root of the file system hierarchy /		
/bin	Essential binaries
/boot	Static boot files
/cdrom	Historical mount point
/dev	Device files
/etc	Configuration files
/home	User home folders
/lib	Library files (32-bit)
/lib64	Library files (64-bit)
/lost+found	Recovered files
/media	Removable media
/mnt	Temporary mount point
/opt	Optional packages
/proc	Kernel and process files
/root	Root user home folder
/run	Application state files
/sbin	System binaries
/srv	Service data
/sys	Virtual file system
/timeshift	Backup files
/tmp	Temporary files
/usr	User binaries
/var	Variable data files

Beware

Do not confuse the /root directory (the home directory of the root superuser) with the / root of the file system.

The purpose of each standard Linux directory is described in more detail on the ensuing pages of this chapter.

Recognizing Directories

/bin
Contains small executable programs (binaries) that are required when your PC boots up, and programs that execute basic commands. This directory is roughly equivalent to the **C:\Windows** directory in Windows.

/boot
Contains important files required when your PC boots up and also the Linux kernel itself – the heart of the operating system. The kernel controls access to all the hardware devices your computer supports, and allows multiple programs to run concurrently and share that hardware.

/cdrom
This is historically a directory in which CD-ROMs inserted into the system were mounted – the standard location is now **/media**.

/dev
Contains special file system entries that represent devices that are attached to the system. These allow programs access to the device drivers that are essential for the system to function properly – although the actual driver files are located elsewhere. The entry **/dev/sda** represents the first hard drive on your PC.

/etc
Contains system configuration files storing information about everything from user passwords and system initialization to screen resolution settings. These are plain text files that can be viewed in a text editor. The files in this directory are roughly equivalent to the combination of **.ini** files and the Registry entries found in the Windows operating system.

/home

Contains a sub-directory for each user account to store personal data files. If there is a user account named "mike" there will be a **/home/mike** directory where that user can store personal files – other users cannot save files there. This directory is where you store all your working documents, images, and media files.

/lib

Contains 32-bit library files that are used by the executable programs in the **/bin** and **/sbin** directories. These shared libraries are particularly important for booting the system and executing commands within the root file system. They are roughly equivalent to the **.dll** (**D**ynamic **L**ink **L**ibraries) in Windows.

/lib64

Contains 64-bit library files that are used by the executable programs in the **/bin** and **/sbin** directories.

/lost+found

Contains misplaced files that may be corrupted, but from which data can still be recovered.

/media

This is a directory in which removable media inserted into the system gets mounted. When you connect a USB flash drive to your PC, a sub-directory, such as **/media/flash-drive**, is created.

/mnt

This is a directory in which the system administrator can temporarily mount an additional file system.

...cont'd

/opt

Contains nothing initially, but this directory provides a special area where optional add-on application software packages can be installed. If "example" is the name of a particular software package in the **/opt** directory, then all its files could be placed within sub-directories of an **/opt/example** directory.

/proc

Contains special files that relay information to and from the kernel. The hierarchy of "virtual" files within this directory represents the current state of the kernel. Unlike binary and text files, most virtual files are listed as zero bytes in size and are time-stamped with the current date and time. This reflects the notion that they are constantly updating.

/root

This is the home directory of the root account superuser – for security reasons, regular users cannot access this directory.

/run

Contains transient files required by applications at runtime to supply data such as process IDs.

/sbin

Contains executable system programs (binaries) that are only used by the root superuser and by Linux when the system is booting up or performing system recovery operations. For instance, the clock program that maintains the system time when Linux is running is located in the **/sbin** directory. This directory is roughly equivalent to the **C:\Windows\system** directory in Windows.

/srv
Contains files that supply data for services provided by the system.

/sys
This is a virtual file system that stores the kernel's view of the system and of the devices connected to the system.

/timeshift
Contains backup snapshots of the system taken at intervals specified by the Timeshift app.

/tmp
Contains temporary files that have been created by running programs. Mostly these are deleted when the program gets closed, but some do get left behind – periodically these should be deleted. This directory is roughly equivalent to the **C:\Windows\Temp** directory in Windows.

/usr
Contains applications and files used by users, as opposed to applications and files used by the system. For example, non-essential applications are located inside the **/usr/bin** directory instead of the **/bin** directory.

/var
Contains variable data files that store information about ongoing system status, particularly logs of system activity. To see recent logged event messages, enter **tail /var/log/syslog** at a prompt.

Navigating with Nemo

The standard Linux sub-directories can be viewed graphically by opening the Nemo file browser app in the / system root location. In Linux Mint, Nemo can be launched by clicking the  "Files" button on the Taskbar or by selecting "Files" on the Menu.

 Click **Menu**, **Accessories**, **Files** to open the file browser – see the sub-directories within your home directory

 Expand the **My Computer list** in the left-hand sidebar

 Click the **File System** item – to see all the system's standard sub-directories within the / system root directory

If you cannot see the sidebar when you open Nemo, hit the F9 key to show the sidebar.

Notice that when you click on a folder icon, information about its contents appears at the bottom of the window – see how many folders are empty.

You can click these buttons to change the sidebar view and to show/hide the sidebar.

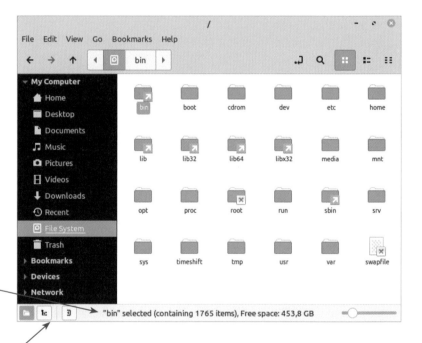

4 Click any directory folder to explore the system's standard sub-directories

5 Click the ← back button above the sidebar to go to the previously-visited location

You can navigate through the file system with Nemo by clicking on a folder or by clicking on a location in the sidebar. Also, you can click the button on the toolbar to open a location field, then type in a directory address and hit the **Enter** key.

 Click the folder icon of the **/home** directory ("home") – there will be a folder there bearing your username

Notice that Nemo displays the name of the currently-displayed directory on its title bar.

 Click on the folder bearing your username to see the contents of your home directory

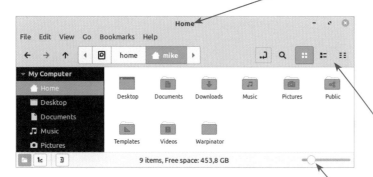

You can click these buttons to change how the folders are viewed.

 On the Nemo file browser toolbar, click the ↑ up button twice to navigate back up to the **/** root location

You can drag this slider to adjust the zoom level.

Click the **Home** item in the sidebar to navigate to the user's home directory once more – then return to / again

Click the button on Nemo's toolbar to reveal the location field, and type the address of the user's home directory (in this case **/home/mike**), then hit **Enter** to navigate to the home directory one more time

Handling Files

All data files you create in Linux should only be saved in your home directory, or a sub-directory ("folder"). They can be revisited at any time using the Nemo file browser and can be easily copied, moved, renamed, or deleted:

 Click on **Menu**, **Accessories**, **Text Editor** to launch a plain text editor, then type in some text and click the Save button on the toolbar (or click the File, Save menu)

 In the "Save As" dialog, double-click your **Documents** folder to open it, then type a name for the text document (say, **sample.txt**) and click the Save button

 Launch the Nemo file browser, then open the **Documents** folder that is located in your home directory and find the saved text file

 Right-click on the file's icon and choose **Copy** from the context menu – to copy that file to the "clipboard"

The **clipboard** is a memory buffer provided by the operating system and is used for short-term data transfer.

Directories may contain hidden files – click the **View**, **Show Hidden Files** menu in the Nemo file browser to also show hidden files.

5 Next, right-click on the **Public** folder within your home directory, then choose **Paste Into Folder** from the context menu – to deposit a copy of the file

6 Open the Public folder, then right-click on the copied file and choose **Rename** from the context menu to see the file name get highlighted – ready to be changed

Hot tip

You can right-click in the file browser and choose **Create New Folder** from the context menu to add a new directory – but remember that this should be within your home directory hierarchy.

7 Now, type a new file name ("copy", for instance), then hit **Return** to rename the file as **copy.txt** – the file extension **.txt** remains

8 Right-click on the renamed file and choose **Cut** from the context menu

9 Navigate back into the Documents folder, then right-click on the file browser window and choose **Paste** from the context menu – depositing the renamed file

10 Drag the mouse pointer across both files, then right-click and choose **Move to Trash** to delete the files

Hot tip

To recover a trashed file, click the **Trash** icon on the file browser's sidebar (or the one on the Desktop), right-click the file icon, then choose the **Restore** option from the context menu.

Creating Shortcuts

It is often convenient to create Desktop shortcuts to the apps and files you access most frequently. Shortcuts for apps can be created from options on the Menu, or from the Desktop context menu. Shortcuts for files can be created as links using the file browser:

 Right-click an app icon on the Menu, then click the **Add to desktop** option to place a shortcut on the Desktop

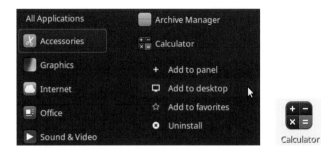

 Right-click anywhere on the Desktop, then choose **Create a new launcher here** from the context menu – to open a "Launcher Properties" dialog box

3 Enter a shortcut Name, then click the **Browse** button to open a "Choose a command" dialog

4 Navigate to the **/usr/bin** directory and select the app for which you want to create a shortcut – to add its path in the Command field

 Click the icon button to open a "Choose an icon" dialog

6 Next, enter **gnome-character-map** in the Search box, then choose an appropriate shortcut icon in the right pane

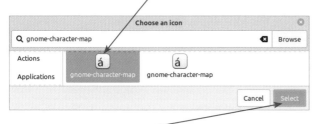

7 Click the **Select** button to close the dialog and see the icon appear in the "Launcher Properties" dialog

8 Click the **OK** button to place a shortcut on the Desktop

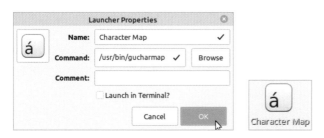

If a selected icon does not appear in the **Launcher Properties** dialog it will not appear on the shortcut – a default icon will appear.

69

9 Open the file browser in your home Documents directory, then right-click on a text file and choose the **Edit, Make Link** menu – a shortcut icon now appears in that directory and has an arrow denoting it to be a link

Care must be taken to maintain links, as changes to the target file, such as renaming or moving it, will leave the links "orphaned" – no longer pointing correctly at the target file.

10 Drag the link icon from the file browser and drop it onto the Desktop to create a shortcut that can be clicked to launch a Text Editor displaying the target file

Link to example.txt

Locating Files

It is important to recognize that many directories in Linux contain hidden sub-directories and hidden files containing configuration data. These are like the "System" files that are hidden by default in the Windows operating system. In Linux, the name of each hidden directory and file always begins with a dot.

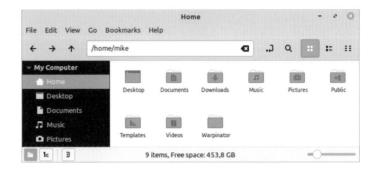

1 Open the file browser in your home directory

2 Now, click **View, Show Hidden Files** to see all contents

Hot tip

Right-click on the file browser window then select **Arrange Items** from the context menu to choose how you would like the contents arranged.

The easiest way to find a file on your system is with the "Search" box in the Nemo file browser. You can find all files of a particular file type by entering a file extension into the Search box. For example, enter **txt** to find all files with a ".txt" file extension.

Conversely, you can find all files of a known name regardless of the file extension by entering a name into the Search box. The file browser begins searching as soon as you enter three characters into the Search box, so you don't need to know the full name, and the letters need not be the first three letters of the name – just three consecutive letters within the name. You can substitute the * wildcard character for unknown letters too. The search is not case-sensitive, so the results will include uppercase and lowercase matches to the name (or part-name) that you enter:

The Search results will not include hidden files.

1 Open the file browser in your home directory

2 Click the Search button on the toolbar

3 Type three characters into the Search box to match a file name or sub-directory within your home directory

You can click the **Favorites** button to save or forget searches, and right-click it to display saved favorites to quickly make a search again.

4 Type three characters in the Search box to match any file type whose file extension ends with "pg"

Understanding Permissions

In Linux, each file and directory has an "Owner" – generally, this is the user who created it. The Owner has full permission to read the file, write to the file, and to execute the file (if it's executable).

The Owner may also set permissions to specify if other users can read, write, and execute the file. The file's accessibility can be restricted to the Owner, or to a "Group" of which the owner is a member, or to any user of the system ("Others").

Permission settings of a file can be found on the Permissions tab of its Properties dialog:

1 Right-click on a file, then choose the **Properties** item from the context menu – to launch the "Properties" dialog

When a user account is created, a **Group** of the same name is also created – of which that user is a member.

You can select the **Emblems** tab to add a symbol to the file icon – for example, denoting the file as important.

72

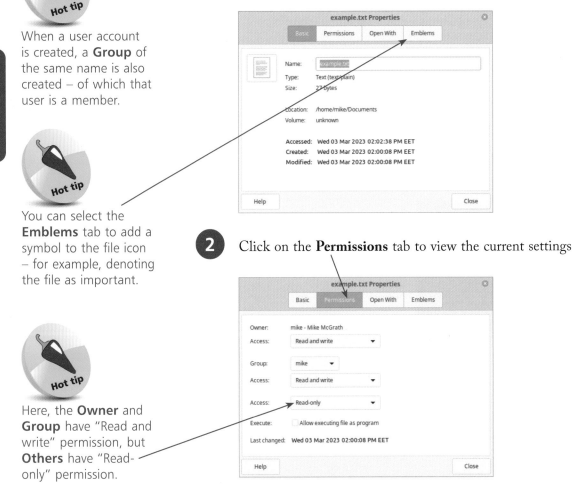

2 Click on the **Permissions** tab to view the current settings

Here, the **Owner** and **Group** have "Read and write" permission, but **Others** have "Read-only" permission.

Usually the Owner, Group and Others will have permission to at least read the file. If you are the owner of the file, the Owner will have permission to write – and to execute the file if it's executable.

As the owner of the file you can use the arrowed buttons to change the access permissions of this file:

 Click the arrowed button in the "Others" field, then choose **None** from the drop-down menu to restrict access to the Owner and Group members

If you need to change permissions on files where you are not the owner, you need root superuser status – see page 164 for details.

Checking this option makes the file executable for those users who have permission to access it.

73

4 Click on the **Open With** tab if you would also like to change the default app that opens this file

Changing the default app is applied to all files of this file type, whereas changing permissions is applied to this file only. Here, the change will make LibreOffice Writer the default app to open all plain text files instead of the Text Editor app.

Summary

- The Linux **file system** comprises a number of standard directories arranged hierarchically beneath the / system root.

- Data files created by a user should only be stored in the **/home** directory structure – in the user's **home** directory.

- A user can navigate around the file system graphically using the **Nemo file browser** app.

- An individual **file** can be copied, moved, renamed, and deleted with the file browser.

- Desktop launcher shortcuts are easily created by selecting the **Add to desktop** option on the Menu.

- The "Launcher Properties" dialog can create shortcuts to apps.

- A shortcut to a local file can be created as a **link**, which is merely a reference to the target file.

- Care must be taken to avoid orphaning links when the target file gets moved or renamed.

- It is important to recognize that many Linux directories contain **hidden** sub-directories and files.

- Hidden files and directories always have names that begin with a **.** (period) character.

- The **View**, **Show Hidden Files** menu in the file browser allows all content to be seen.

- Files can be located using the file browser's **Search** box to match file names or file extensions.

- The owner of a file can specify access permissions to allow the **Owner**, **Group**, and **Others** to read, write, and execute.

5 Engaging the Internet

Browsing the Web

Most Linux distros include the open-source Mozilla Firefox web browser. This popular free browser is available for various platforms and is highly customizable. It has been developed by the open-source community from original Netscape browser source code into a strongly standards-compliant product:

1 Ensure you are connected to the internet, then click **Menu**, **Internet**, **Firefox Web Browser** to launch the web browser at its "Start Page"

Close tab   New tab   Address bar   Add bookmark   Bookmarks & History   Show/Hide sidebar

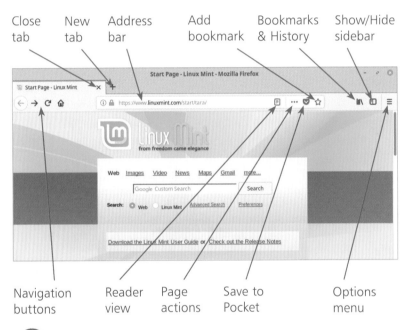

Navigation buttons   Reader view   Page actions   Save to Pocket   Options menu

Hot tip

You can enter a URL in the address bar and hit **Return** to visit a web page. The address bar is also a Search box for the Yahoo! search engine.

Hot tip

The **Save to Pocket** feature lets you save web pages so you can view them later on any device.

2 Click the **+ New Tab** button to open a new tab containing a Search box and links to "Top Sites"

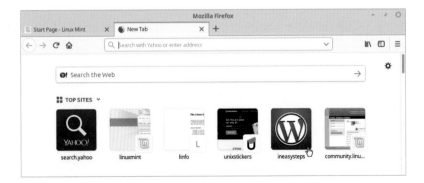

3 Search for an item of interest, such as "How solar cells work", then select a link from the results to visit the page

Reader view button
Show sidebars button

The **Reader view** button is not available for all web pages, but when visible it toggles between views. Click it to return to the regular page view.

4 Next, click the **Reader view** button on the toolbar to see the page without distractions

5 Now, click the **Add bookmark** button on the toolbar, then choose the **Bookmarks Toolbar** folder option

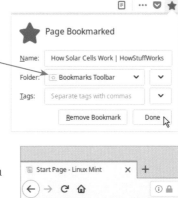

Click the **Show sidebars** button and choose the **Bookmarks** option to see your bookmarks appear in the sidebar.

6 Click the **Done** button to see the item now appear on a "Bookmarks Toolbar" so you can revisit the page

Customizing Firefox

The interface of the Firefox web browser is highly customizable and you can install "add-ons" for extra functionality:

 Right-click on the toolbar, then choose the **Customize** option on the context menu – to open a "Customize Firefox" window

2 Drag any item onto the toolbar to add it, or drag an item onto the Customize Firefox menu to remove it

Hot tip

You can also drag items onto the **Overflow Menu**, which you can access later by clicking the toolbar's **>>** button.

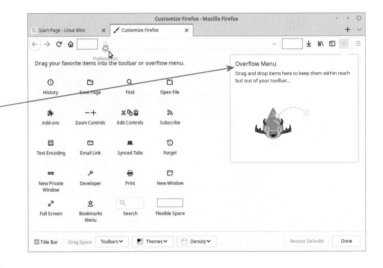

3 Click the **Themes** button and choose from the "My Themes" list of installed themes, or click on **Get More Themes** to install additional themes

4 See your chosen theme instantly applied to the Firefox interface

Hot tip

Click the **Toolbars** button to add or remove more toolbars, and click the **Density** button to adjust the size of the toolbar icons.

5 Next, click the **Manage** button on the My Themes list to open an "Add-ons Manager" window

You can also use the Add-ons Manager to remove add-ons later.

6 Enter the name of an add-on into the Search box, such as "Adblock Plus", then hit the **Enter** key

7 Select the link for "Adblock Plus" on the Search results page, then click the **Add to Firefox** button to install it

Adblock Plus is a top-rated free add-on with over 11 million users. It automatically blocks advertisements and puts a button on the Firefox toolbar. This displays the number of ads blocked and provides options to allow non-intrusive ads.

8 Now, click **Add** to give permissions and install the add-on into Firefox

79

Exchanging Email

Many Linux distros include the popular Thunderbird email app. The first time Thunderbird gets started it offers you a new email account or the option to use an existing email account. Typically, you will need to supply the name of your ISP's mail servers (POP and SMTP), and your email address and password. When this is complete, and you have an internet connection, you can start sending and receiving email messages:

 Click **Menu**, **Internet**, **Thunderbird Mail**, then click the **Get Messages** button on Thunderbird's toolbar

 Expand the folders list in the left-hand pane, then click the **Inbox** to see received messages in the top right-hand pane

Thunderbird is also a contact manager. Right-click this "From" field and choose **Add to Address Book** then click the **Address Book** button on the toolbar to see your contacts list.

The POP (**P**ost **O**ffice **P**rotocol) server handles incoming emails, and the SMTP (**S**imple **M**ail **T**ransfer **P**rotocol) server handles outgoing emails.

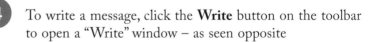 Click on a received message in the top right-hand pane to see its contents appear in the bottom right-hand pane

 To write a message, click the **Write** button on the toolbar to open a "Write" window – as seen opposite

⑤ In the Write window's **From** field, select the account from which to send the message

 In the **To** field, type the email address you are sending to

⑦ In the **Subject** field, type a short message title

80

8 Now, type your message in the main window

9 Use the options on the formatting bar to adjust the font, layout, content, and insert a **Smiley face** emoji

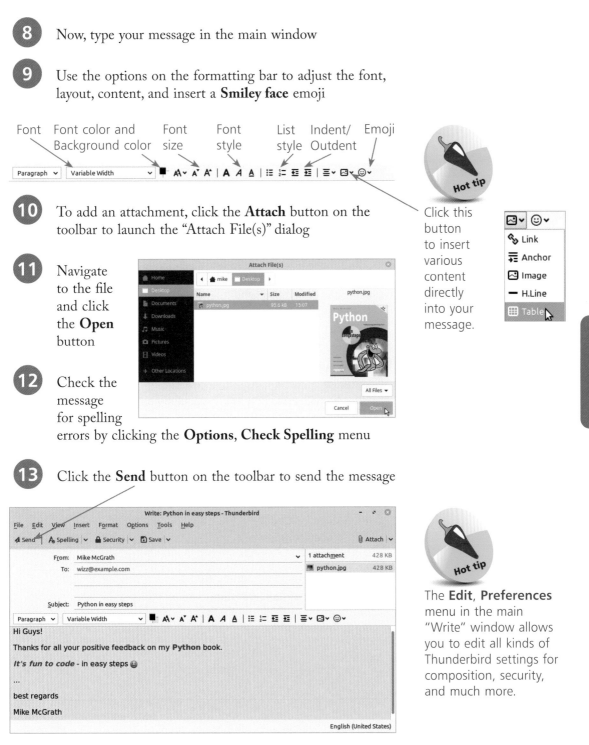

Font | Font color and Background color | Font size | Font style | List style | Indent/ Outdent | Emoji

Paragraph ▾ | Variable Width ▾

10 To add an attachment, click the **Attach** button on the toolbar to launch the "Attach File(s)" dialog

11 Navigate to the file and click the **Open** button

12 Check the message for spelling errors by clicking the **Options**, **Check Spelling** menu

13 Click the **Send** button on the toolbar to send the message

Hot tip

Click this button to insert various content directly into your message.

🔗 Link
⎯⎯ Anchor
🖼 Image
— H.Line
⊞ Table

81

Hot tip

The **Edit**, **Preferences** menu in the main "Write" window allows you to edit all kinds of Thunderbird settings for composition, security, and much more.

Chatting Online

Linux distros typically include a cross-platform instant messaging application. Linux Mint includes the free open-source HexChat IRC (**I**nternet **R**elay **C**hat) app. This can be used to chat about Linux and other topics on the "freenode" IRC network:

1 Click **Menu**, **Internet**, **HexChat** to launch the app – connecting to the "Official Linux Mint Support Channel"

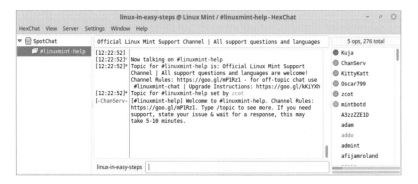

2 Next, click the **HexChat**, **Network List** menu option – to open the "Network List" dialog

3 Enter a **Nick name** and a **User name**, then select the "freenode" network

4 Now, click the **Connect** button – to connect to the "freenode" network

5 Once connected, enter the command **/join ##Linux** in the HexChat text field – to join freenode's Linux Support Channel

The **Nick name** will be your name visible in the IRC channels and the **User name** is your identity to the server.

...cont'd

If the "User List" is not visible, click the **View**, **User List** menu options to make it appear.

6 Enter comments or questions in the HexChat text field to chat with other users connected to this channel

7 Double-click on any user in the **User List** to switch to a "Dialog with" window to chat directly with that user

8 Click the **Chat** button to send a chat request to that user

9 Wait until the user accepts the request, then begin to chat

You can click the **Send** button to send a file to the user, and click the **WhoIs** button to see user connection details.

Downloading Content

Linux distros typically include the Transmission BitTorrent Client app to acquire content via the BitTorrent protocol. This lets you download directly from other groups of people – in which each person is called a "peer". Pieces of content from various peers are automatically assembled, making the BitTorrent protocol very efficient and reliable, particularly for large content files.

The Transmission BitTorrent Client first requires you to download a "torrent file" containing information about the content you wish to acquire. These can be found in a BitTorrent directory such as Public Domain Torrents (**publicdomaintorrents.info**), Internet Archive (**archive.org**), or Legit Torrents (**legittorrents.info**):

 Open the **Firefox** web browser and visit a BitTorrent directory, then select an item you would like to download

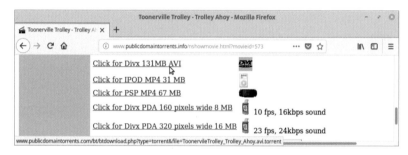

Hot tip

Torrent downloads are often associated with illegal downloads, but free open content can be legally downloaded.

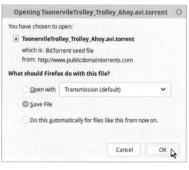

2 Choose to save the torrent file – by default to the **Downloads** folder within your home directory

Hot tip

The first time you launch the **Transmission** app a dialog will appear in which you need to agree to share content responsibly.

3 Click **Menu**, **Internet**, **Transmission** to launch the app

 Click the **Open** button on the Transmission toolbar – to open an "Open a Torrent" dialog

5 Select the torrent file you downloaded and check the **Show options dialog** option

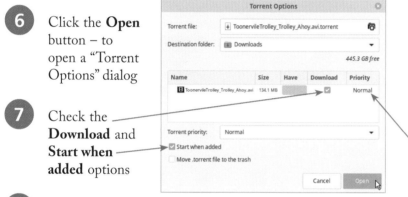

6 Click the **Open** button – to open a "Torrent Options" dialog

7 Check the **Download** and **Start when added** options

Hot tip

You can download multiple torrents simultaneously and click here to set each one's priority to **Low**, **Normal**, or **High**.

8 Click the **Open** button to start downloading the content

Hot tip

Click the **Edit**, **Preferences** menu to specify how your downloads should be managed.

Getting More Apps

In addition to the apps that are supplied with your Linux distro, there are many more free apps that can be easily installed. The Linux Mint distro includes a Software Manager utility app that lets you search for more apps by name or by category. When you select an app, there is a description and screenshot accompanied by user reviews that help you decide if you want to install that app:

 Click **Menu**, **Administration**, **Software Manager** to launch the utility

 Click a category button for the type of app you are seeking – for example, to find a picture editor app, click the **Graphics** button

 Click any item listed in your chosen category to see a description and reviews of that app

You can click this link to open the app's Home page in your web browser and discover more about the app.

4 Click the **Install** button if you decide you want this app

5 Enter your password to download and install the app

The description page of an installed app has a **Remove** button (in place of the **Install** button) that you can click to uninstall that app.

6 Now, click **Menu**, **Graphics** to see a launcher has been added into the appropriate category

Summary

- The **Mozilla Firefox** web browser is included with most Linux distros.

- The **+ New Tab** button in Firefox opens a new tab containing a Search box and links to "Top Sites".

- Firefox provides **Reader view** to hide page distractions.

- Firefox web browser is highly customizable and allows the installation of **add-ons** for extra functionality.

- Many Linux distros include the **Thunderbird** app with which to send and receive email messages.

- The **formatting bar** in Thunderbird allows you to adjust the font, layout, and content, and to insert emojis in your message.

- The **Thunderbird** email app is also a contact manager.

- Linux Mint includes the **HexChat** cross-platform instant messaging app.

- The **Official Linux Mint Support Channel** is available to chat about Linux topics.

- The **Transmission** app can download content using the BitTorrent protocol.

- Transmission requires a **torrent file** containing information about the content to be acquired.

- Pieces of content from various **peers** are automatically assembled, making the BitTorrent protocol very efficient.

- Linux Mint includes a **Software Manager** utility app that groups available apps by category.

- Software Manager provides a **description** and **reviews** of each available app.

- The Software Manager app can **Install** and **Remove** apps from the system.

6 Producing with Office

Creating Documents

The LibreOffice suite that is included with most Linux distros contains a set of office tools similar to those in Microsoft Office: word processor, spreadsheet, and presentation programs, together with a program to create charts, graphs and diagrams, and a database app. If you are familiar with Microsoft Office you will feel instantly at home with the LibreOffice equivalents.

Most importantly, LibreOffice contains file filters that allow it to work with standard Microsoft Office documents from Word, Excel and PowerPoint. Files can be saved in Microsoft Office file formats, as well as formats native to LibreOffice, and objects (OLE objects, plugins, video, applets, charts) can be embedded within a document in much the same way as in Microsoft Word:

Hot tip

LibreOffice is forked from OpenOffice, which was based on original code from the StarOffice application by Sun MicroSystems. Sun made the code freely available for development by the open-source community – so LibreOffice has no proprietary ties.

Hot tip

There are versions of LibreOffice for Linux, Mac and Windows – all available for free download at libreoffice.org

1 Click **Menu, Office, LibreOffice Writer** to launch a word processor with a new blank document open

2 Type some content in the new document

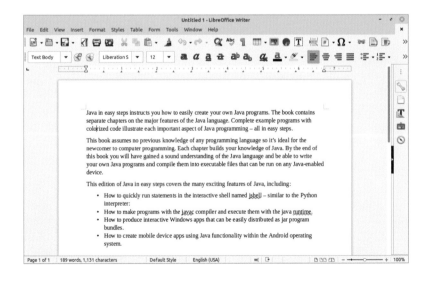

3 Click the **Edit, Select All** menu item (or press **Ctrl + A**) to select all content, then choose a font from this drop-down list on the toolbar

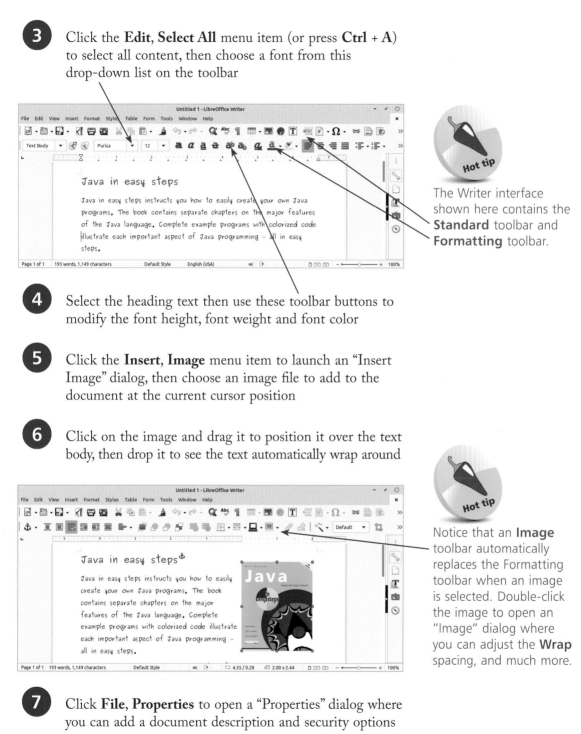

The Writer interface shown here contains the **Standard** toolbar and **Formatting** toolbar.

4 Select the heading text then use these toolbar buttons to modify the font height, font weight and font color

5 Click the **Insert, Image** menu item to launch an "Insert Image" dialog, then choose an image file to add to the document at the current cursor position

6 Click on the image and drag it to position it over the text body, then drop it to see the text automatically wrap around

Notice that an **Image** toolbar automatically replaces the Formatting toolbar when an image is selected. Double-click the image to open an "Image" dialog where you can adjust the **Wrap** spacing, and much more.

7 Click **File, Properties** to open a "Properties" dialog where you can add a document description and security options

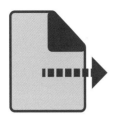

Exporting Documents

When saving documents from the LibreOffice word processor, the default file format used is the ODF (**O**pen **D**ocument **F**ormat) Text format (**.odt**). Many alternative file formats are available, however, so your documents can be made compatible with Microsoft Office:

 Click **File**, **Save** (or press **Ctrl + S**) to launch the "Save" dialog, then type a document name in the **Name** field

 Click the arrowed file type button to open a list of possible formats in which to save the document – choose the format **Word 2007-365 (.docx)**

 Choose a location at which to save the document, such as your Documents folder, then click the **Save** button

Hot tip

In the **Save** dialog you don't need to include a file extension in the Name field – it gets added automatically.

 If a "Confirm File Format" dialog appears, click the button to confirm you wish to save using the **.docx** file format – the file is then saved at the chosen location

LibreOffice Writer has built-in support for the PDF (**P**ortable **D**ocument **F**ormat) format. This allows you to create read-only versions of your documents in the popular PDF format, without any additional software. The PDF format maintains the style and content of the original document in a very compact file that can be easily transferred around networks and the internet:

 Click **File, Export As, Export as PDF** to open a "PDF Options" dialog

 Select **All** for the "Range" option, then click the **Export** button to create a PDF version of the document – with the same file name but with a **.pdf** file extension

 Copy the documents created in LibreOffice on Linux to a Windows system for comparison in Microsoft Word

Don't forget

The uneditable PDF version maintains its appearance precisely, but the editable DOCX version may substitute a different font if the original is not also installed in Windows – more importantly, both versions maintain color and layout formatting.

Creating Spreadsheets

The spreadsheet app that is part of the free LibreOffice suite provides the powerful ability to perform calculations on data entries using given formulas. It also allows spreadsheets to be saved in the format compatible with Microsoft Excel (**.xlsx**):

1 Click **Menu**, **Office**, **LibreOffice Calc** to launch the spreadsheet app with a new blank spreadsheet open

2 Enter some row and column headings, then use the **Font Color** button to accent their purpose

lunch.xls - LibreOffice Calc

File Edit View Insert Format Styles Sheet Data Tools Window Help

B5:H10

	A	B	C	D	E	F	G	H	I
1									
2		School lunch costs							
3									
4		Monday	Tuesday	Wednesday	Thursday	Friday	Total	Average	
5	Week 1								
6	Week 2								
7	Week 3								
8	Week 4								
9	Total								
10	Average								
11									

3 Drag over all cells that will contain data, then right-click and choose **Format Cells** from the context menu – to open a "Format Cells" dialog

4 Choose the **Currency** category in the dialog, then click the dialog's **OK** button to apply the selection

Format Cells

Numbers Font Font Effects Alignment Asian Typography Borders Background Cell Protection

Category	Format	Language
Number	USD $ English (USA)	Default - English (USA)
Percent		
Currency	-$1,234.00	
Date	-$1,234	
Time	-$1,234.00	
Scientific	-$1,234.--	
Fraction	-1,234.00 USD	
Boolean Value	-1,234.00 USD	
Text	-$1,234	$2.70
	-$1,234.00	

5 Enter numerical values in all cells for each week row and day column – each value is treated as a currency amount

You can choose cell colors, fonts, borders, alignment, and more in the **Format Cells** dialog.

6 Drag the mouse across each day cell on a row and its "Total" cell, then click the Σ button on the toolbar and select **SUM** – a **SUM** formula appears in the formula field and a row total value appears in the Total cell

7 Repeat the previous step for each row and column

G9	▼	*fx* Σ =	=SUM(G5:G8)					
	A	B	C	D	E	F	G	H
1								
2		School lunch costs						
3								
4		Monday	Tuesday	Wednesday	Thursday	Friday	Total	Average
5	Week 1	$2.70	$2.30	$2.50	$2.65	$2.90	$13.05	$2.61
6	Week 2	$2.75	$2.20	$2.40	$2.00	$2.60	$11.95	$2.39
7	Week 3	$2.70	$2.70	$2.70	$2.25	$2.35	$12.70	$2.54
8	Week 4	$2.70	$2.70	$2.60	$2.70	$2.20	$12.90	$2.58
9	Total	$10.85	$9.90	$10.20	$9.60	$10.05	$50.60	
10	Average							

Hot tip

You can use the **Background Color** button to accent the purpose of each cell.

8 Type **=AVERAGE** in an "Average" cell at a row end and hit **Return**, then drag across the day cells on that row and hit **Return** again – a row average appears in the Average cell

9 Repeat the previous step for each row and column

H10	▼	*fx* Σ =	=AVERAGE(H5:H8)					
	A	B	C	D	E	F	G	H
1								
2		School lunch costs						
3								
4		Monday	Tuesday	Wednesday	Thursday	Friday	Total	Average
5	Week 1	$2.70	$2.30	$2.50	$2.65	$2.90	$13.05	$2.61
6	Week 2	$2.75	$2.20	$2.40	$2.00	$2.60	$11.95	$2.39
7	Week 3	$2.70	$2.70	$2.70	$2.25	$2.35	$12.70	$2.54
8	Week 4	$2.70	$2.70	$2.60	$2.70	$2.20	$12.90	$2.58
9	Total	$10.85	$9.90	$10.20	$9.60	$10.05	$50.60	
10	Average	$2.71	$2.48	$2.55	$2.40	$2.51		$2.53

Hot tip

You can open this file in Excel on a Windows system to see that all formatting and formula functions are preserved.

10 Click **File, Save** (or press **Ctrl + S**) to launch the "Save" dialog, then type a spreadsheet name in the **Name** field

11 Click the arrowed file type button to open a list of possible formats in which to save the spreadsheet – accept the default ODF Spreadsheet format (**.ods**) or choose the format **Excel 2007-365 (.xlsx)**

Creating Presentations

The presentation app that is part of the free LibreOffice suite provides the ability to easily produce great slideshows. It also allows presentations to be saved in the format compatible with Microsoft PowerPoint (**.ppt**).

 Click **Menu, Office, LibreOffice Impress** to launch the app with a new blank presentation open

 A "Select a Template" dialog should also appear when you launch the app – select a template, such as **Lights**

Hot tip

If the "Select a Template" dialog does not appear when you launch the app, click the **File, Close** menu to close the blank presentation, then select **Templates** in the "backstage" window.

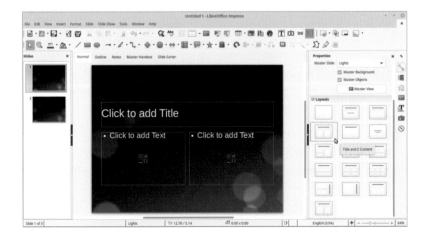

 Select how you want the content grouped from an option in the "Layouts" pane, such as **Title and 2 Content**

Hot tip

If the "Layouts" pane is not immediately visible, click **View, Slide Layout** to make it appear.

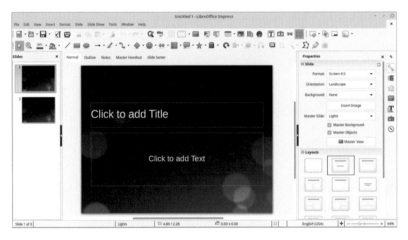

4 Click on the "Click to add Title" box, then type a title

5 Click **Format**, **Align**, **Center** to position the title

6 Next, type some narrative text in the left "Click to add Text" box

7 Click on the right "Click to add Text" box, then click **Insert**, **Image** to launch an "Insert Image" dialog

8 Choose an appropriate image to add to the slide, then use the grab handles around the image to adjust its size to your liking

9 Right-click this slide in the "Slides" pane, then choose **New Slide** to add a slide with the same template and layout – make further slides to complete the presentation

10 Click **Slideshow, Start from First Slide** (or press **F5**) to run the presentation

11 Click **File, Save** (or press **Ctrl + S**) to launch the "Save" dialog, then type a presentation name in the **Name** field

12 Click the arrowed file type button to open a list of possible formats – accept the default ODF Presentation format (**.odp**) or choose **PowerPoint 2007-365 (.pptx)**

You can switch to "Master Slide View" where you can add elements you want to appear on all slides. Slides you have created are not visible when in Master Slide View, so it looks like they have disappeared. Click **View**, **Normal** to continue working on your slides.

If the "Slides" pane is not immediately visible, click **View**, **Slide Pane** to make it appear.

Creating Visualizations

The LibreOffice suite includes an accomplished drawing tool that can be launched from any LibreOffice app to quickly create drawings, charts, diagrams and graphs:

1 From any LibreOffice app, click **File**, **New**, **Drawing** or click **Menu**, **Office**, **LibreOffice Draw** to launch the app

2 Click the arrowed button beside the **Basic Shapes** button on the Drawing toolbar, then choose the rounded rectangle object from the selection offered

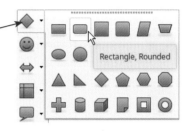

3 Drag the mouse in the drawing area to create a rectangle and press **Ctrl** + **C** to copy the object, then press **Ctrl** + **V** five times to paste five more rectangles on top of the first

4 Drag the rectangles to separate areas, then click the **Connector** button on the Drawing toolbar

5 Click on a rectangle, then drag to another rectangle to create connecting lines

6 Now, click the **T** **Insert Text box** button and label the rectangles

Hot tip

If the Drawings toolbar is not immediately visible, click **View**, **Toolbars**, **Drawing** to make it appear.

98

Don't forget

Drawings can be saved in the native ODF (**O**pen **D**ocument **F**ormat), Drawing format (**.odg**), or exported in a variety of image formats such as PNG (**.png**), GIF (**.gif**), and SVG (**.svg**).

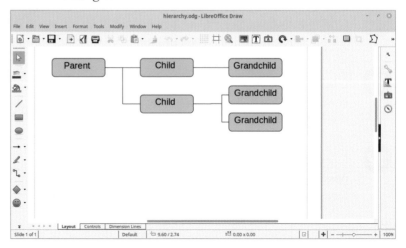

7 Click the **Insert,
Chart** menu to add
a default bar chart
to the drawing
area – a chart
Formatting toolbar
also appears

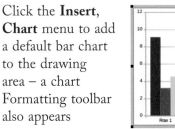

8 On the Formatting menu, click the 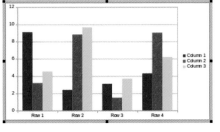 **Data Table**
button and modify the default values in the "Data Table"
dialog that appears, then close that dialog

The chart Formatting
toolbar can be launched
from the **View,
Toolbars**, menu – after
you have inserted a
chart.

9 Click the
Chart Type
button to launch
a "Chart Type"
dialog, then
choose **Line** in
the left-hand
pane and **Points
and Lines** as
the type of chart

99

10 Click the **OK** button to close the "Chart Type" dialog
and apply the chosen line style

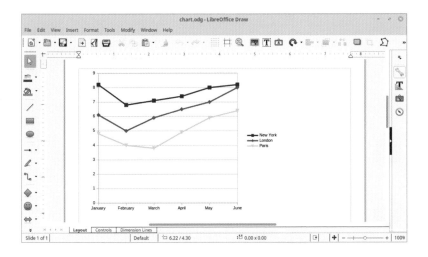

To insert an existing
chart into a document,
click **Insert, Object,
OLE Object** – but
to insert the default
editable chart, just click
Insert, Chart.

Running Macros

A "macro" is a recorded sequence of keystrokes that are stored with a given name. Running a macro replays the sequence, writing into the current document. This is particularly useful for recreating frequently-typed text within spreadsheets in LibreOffice Calc and within text documents in LibreOffice Writer:

 Launch Writer, then click **Tools**, **Options**, **LibreOffice**, **Advanced** and check the **Enable macro recording** option

Hot tip

A Java Runtime Environment (JRE) is required on the Linux system to run macros. Linux Mint includes the OpenJDK Runtime Environment for Java, but you may need to install a Java Runtime Environment on other distros.

 Next, click **Tools**, **Macros**, **Record Macro** to begin recording – a small window appears, bearing a **Stop Recording** button

 Click the ≡ **Center** button on the toolbar, then type your address

100 Main Street
Springfield

 Click the **Stop Recording** button in the small window, then see a "Basic Macros" dialog appear

In the **Macro Name** text field, replace the name "Main" by the name "Address", then click the **Save** button

6 To run this macro at any time, first click **Tools**, **Macros**, **Run Macro** to launch a "Macro Selector" dialog

7 Select the Address macro from **My Macros**, **Standard**, **Module1**, then click the **Run** button to write your address

The macro recorder only records actions relating to document content in the window where it was started, and it only works with the LibreOffice Writer and Calc apps.

8 To edit this macro, click **Tools**, **Macros**, **Edit Macros** to launch a "My Macros" dialog, then select the Address macro to see the code behind the macro actions

9 Locate the text values describing your address, then replace them with different values and click **File**, **Save** to apply the changes

10 Finally, repeat Steps 6 and 7 to run this macro once more and see the modified address values written

Click on **Tools**, **Macros**, **Organize Macros**, **LibreOffice Basic**, then select an existing macro and use the **Delete** button to remove it.

Adding Interaction

LibreOffice apps allow interactive "form" controls to be added to documents – much like those found in web forms. These allow the user to quickly produce a finished document by providing minimal input, and this is particularly useful when repeatedly producing the same document with differing data:

1 In LibreOffice Writer, click **View**, **Toolbars**, **Form Controls** to open a "Form Controls" dialog, then click its **Design Mode** button to set it to "On" – so form controls can be added

2 Click the **Label Field** button on the "Form Controls" dialog, then drag the mouse on the document to create three labels – by default, these will each contain the text "Label Field"

3 Double-click on each label in turn to open its "Properties" dialog, and change the value of each **Label** property, then hit **Return** to see the label text change

	Properties: Label Field	
⚓		
Airport:	General Events	
Flight:	Name....................	Label Field 1
	Label.....................	Airport:
Arrival Date:	Enabled................	Yes
	Visible..................	Yes
	Printable...............	Yes
	Anchor.................	To Paragraph
	PositionX.............	0.44 "
	PositionY.............	0.44 "
	Width...................	1.48 "

Hot tip

Right-click on a control, select **Position and Size** from the context menu, and choose **Anchor**, **To Paragraph** from the dialog that appears to allow easier positioning of the control.

4 Click the [ABI] **Text Box** button on the controls dialog, then drag the mouse on the document to create two text boxes

5 Click the **Date Field** button in the "Form Controls" dialog, then drag the mouse to create a date field box

6 Double-click the date field box to open its "Properties" dialog, then set its **Drop-down** property to "Yes" and its **Date Format** property to "Standard (long)"

7 Now, click the **Design Mode** button to set it to "Off", then enter data in the text boxes and use the **Drop-down** menu to choose a date

Airport	Melbourne, Tullamarine
Flight	American Airlines AA7356
Arrival Date	Wednesday, April 12, 2023

The data entered into form fields can be edited later to produce new completed forms.

8 Save the file, then click **File, Export As, Export as PDF** to create a version that can be sent to others

Handling Data

The LibreOffice suite includes a database app that, like Microsoft Access, lets you store data and easily extract specific items of data:

 Click **Menu**, **Office**, **LibreOffice Base** to launch the app, then select "Create a new database" and click **Finish** – to open a "Save" dialog

 Enter a **Name**, then click **Save** to close the dialog

 Select **Tables**, then click **Use Wizard to Create Table** – to open a "Table Wizard" dialog

 Choose the **Personal** category, then select a **Sample table** – to see the available fields within that table

 Click an available field, then click the > button to move it to the **Selected fields** pane – to include it in your table

Select all the fields you want, then click **Finish** to close the dialog and see a "Table Data View" window appear

7 Enter and save your data, then close the window

 8 Select **Queries**, then click **Use Wizard to Create Query** – to open a "Query Wizard" dialog

Library - BooksDatabase - Table Data View

File   Edit   View   Insert   Tools   Window   Help

ID	Title	Genre
1	Coding for Beginners	Programming
2	HTML	Web Design
3	Python	Programming
4	CSS	Web Design
5	PHP	Programming

Hot tip

There is a "Report Wizard" that can quickly produce a summary of your data.

 9 Click the **>>** button to select all fields, then click **Next**

10 **Select Search conditions**, then choose a field to query

Query Wizard

Steps

1. Field selection
2. Sorting order
3. Search conditions
4. Detail or summary
5. Grouping
6. Grouping conditions
7. Aliases
8. Overview

Select the search conditions

○ Match all of the following
○ Match any of the following

Fields	Condition	Value
Library.Genre ▼	is equal to ▼	Programming

Fields	Condition	Value
▼	is equal to ▼	

Help   < Back   Next >   Finish   Cancel

Don't forget

You can specify other conditions, such as **Greater than** for numerical values, and you can specify multiple conditions for finer-precision queries.

105

11 Enter a value to match within the chosen field, then click the **Finish** button – see that a query icon gets added in the app's "Queries" pane

 12 Double-click the query icon to see the results in a "Table Data View" window – extracting only specific data

Queries

Query_Library

Query_Library - BooksDatabase - Table Data View

File   Edit   View   Insert   Tools   Window   Help

ID	Title	Genre
	Coding for Beginners	Programming
3	Python	Programming
5	PHP	Programming

Hot tip

There is also a "Form Wizard" that can quickly produce a user form for data entry.

Summary

- **LibreOffice** contains a set of office tools similar to those in the Microsoft Office suite.

- Files can be saved in **Microsoft Office file formats** and file formats native to LibreOffice apps.

- LibreOffice **Writer** is a word processor app for documents that can contain text and embedded objects.

- LibreOffice Writer has built-in support for the **Portable Document Format (PDF)**.

- LibreOffice **Calc** is a spreadsheet app that can perform calculations on data entries using given formulas.

- LibreOffice Calc provides a **Format Cells** facility to specify how cell content should appear.

- LibreOffice **Impress** is a presentation app that can produce slideshows.

- LibreOffice Impress provides a number of standard **Templates** and offers many standard **Layouts**.

- LibreOffice **Draw** is a drawing app that can create illustrations, charts, diagrams, and graphs.

- LibreOffice Draw provides a **Chart Type** facility that provides many standard charts.

- A **macro** is a recorded sequence of keystrokes that can be replayed to repeat those keystrokes.

- LibreOffice apps can add **form controls** to a document for interaction with the user.

- LibreOffice **Base** is a database app that can store data and retrieve specific items of data.

- LibreOffice Base provides wizards that can create **Tables** and perform **Queries** in a database.

7 Enjoying Media

Viewing Images

Many Linux distros include the simple Image Viewer app (**xviewer**) that can zoom and scroll. In Linux Mint you can find its launcher on the menu in the Accessories category, but usually you will launch it from a right-click context menu:

 Drag the mouse over image file icons to select them, then right-click and choose **Open with Image Viewer**

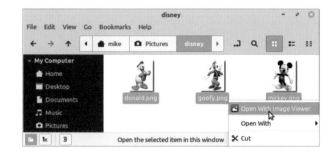

Hot tip

You can also double-click on any file icon to instantly open that image in Image Viewer.

Hot tip

You can use your mouse to zoom too. Place the cursor over an image in Image Viewer then use the mouse wheel to zoom in and out.

 See the Image Viewer app launch, displaying the first image alphabetically

Back/Forward   Zoom In/Out   Full Size   Fit To Window   Rotate Left/Right

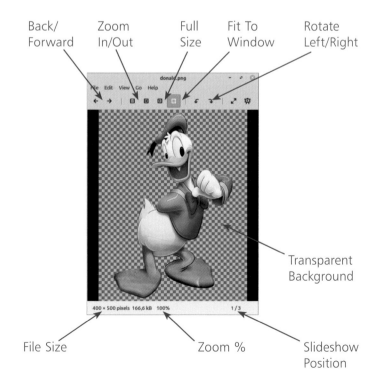

Transparent Background

File Size   Zoom %   Slideshow Position

3 Click the → **Forward** button to view all the selected images, or click **View**, **Slideshow** to view them full-screen

4 Click **View**, **Image Gallery** to open a scrollable gallery pane within the Image Viewer window

5 Scroll to an image, then click **File**, **Set as Wallpaper** to make that image your Desktop background

Managing Photos

In addition to the simple Image Viewer app described on pages 108-109, Linux Mint includes the Pix viewer app that enables you to arrange images and photos in catalogs:

 Click **Menu**, **Graphics**, **Pix** to launch the app, then select an image folder in the left-hand pane to see the photos inside

Navigation   Print   Fullscreen &   Edit   View
              & Find   Slideshow   File   Properties

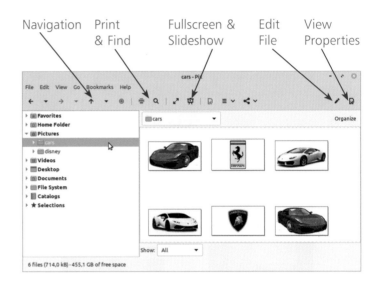

Hot tip

The Pix app starts in **Browser mode**. Double-click on a photo to open it in **Viewer mode**, as shown below.

 Hold down the **Ctrl** key, then click on photos to select them for inclusion in a catalog

 Right-click and select **Tags** from the context menu – to open an "*n* **files**" dialog

Hot tip

The context menu also has options for **Add to Selection**, **Add to Catalog**, and **Comment**.

Descriptive comments can be saved within a photo file as "metadata".

 Enter a tag name and click "Create tag", then click the **Save and Close** button – to tag the selected photos

...cont'd

5 Next, click the **Organize** button just above the photos – to open an "Organize Files" dialog

You can click the **Edit File** button to see lots of quick editing options.

- ◑ Adjust Contrast
- 🎨 Adjust Colors...
- 💧 Enhance Focus...
- 📊 Equalize
- 🖼 Grayscale...
- ▱ Negative

6 Select "Tag" in the drop-down menu, then click the **Execute** button

7 Check the **Create** option beside the tag name you have assigned to the selected photos

8 Click the **Save** button to create the new catalog and close the dialog

The Pix app can automatically open an "Import" dialog when you connect a digital camera or memory card containing photos.

9 Expand **Catalogs**, **Tags** in the left-hand pane of the Pix window, then click on any catalog icon to see its photos

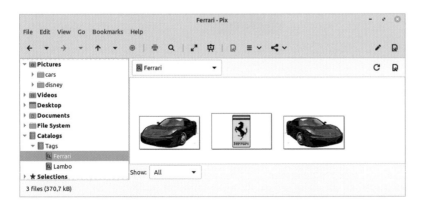

Scanning Images

Linux Mint includes a Document Scanner app that, as its name suggests, makes it simple to import images from a scanner:

1 Connect a scanner to your PC and switch the scanner on

2 Click **Menu**, **Graphics**, **Document Scanner** to launch the app and see it automatically identify your scanner

Hot tip

The **Scan** button changes to a **Stop** button when scanning is in progress – so you can click it to abort the current scan.

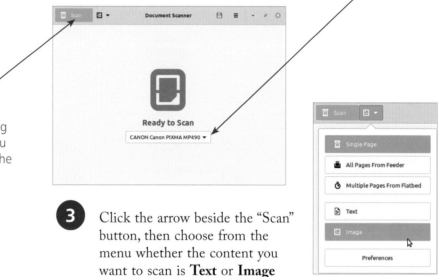

3 Click the arrow beside the "Scan" button, then choose from the menu whether the content you want to scan is **Text** or **Image**

4 Now, click the **Scan** button to scan your content – see the image of the content gradually appear in the app window

Hot tip

Click the ☰ button to open a menu, then select **Preferences**, **Quality** to specify resolution, brightness, and contrast settings.

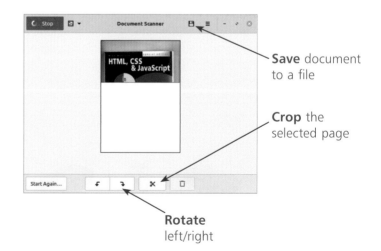

Save document to a file

Crop the selected page

Rotate left/right

5 Click the **Crop** button to see a frame appear over the image, then drag the frame's edges to the desired position

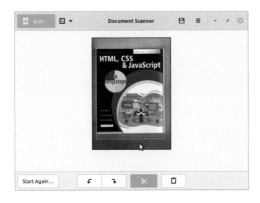

6 Next, click the app's **Save** button to open a "Save As" dialog, then choose a file format from this menu

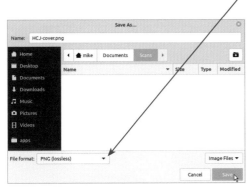

7 Next, click the dialog's **Save** button to import the cropped scan to an image file

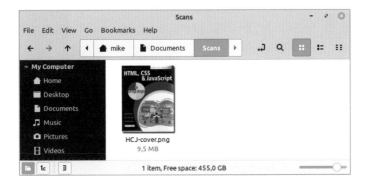

Hot tip

Click the ☰ button to open a menu, then select **Preferences**, **Scanning** to choose a scanner if there is more than one connected.

Hot tip

Multiple scans can be made to add pages in the Document Scanner. Click the ☰ button, then choose **Reorder Pages** to see options for how to rearrange them.

Don't forget

You can double-click the image file to view it in the Image Viewer app.

Editing Images

The primary image editing application in Linux is the GIMP (**G**NU **I**mage **M**anipulation **P**rogram) open-source app that includes over 220 plugins in a standard installation. These provide the GIMP with many of the capabilities of Adobe Photoshop but do not provide native support for CMYK colors.

The GIMP is highly configurable and has powerful scripting support. GIMP can be used to edit images and to create attractive web page graphics:

Main Toolbox   Image Window   Brushes, Patterns and Fonts

Tool Options   Layers, Channels and Paths

Hot tip

The GIMP app is not bundled with Linux Mint by default. See pages 86-87 for installation instructions.

1 Items in the Tool Options panel change according to which tool is selected in the Toolbox panel. For example, click the Paintbrush tool in the Toolbox to see options available for that tool in the Tool Options panel

2 Now, in the Toolbox, select each tool in turn to see their available options in the Tool Options panel

3 The Brushes, Patterns and Fonts panel has tabs for each category that display items in a scrollable window. Each tab displays the current selection for that category. For example, click the 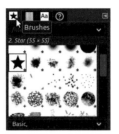 Brushes tab and select a star-shaped brush to see that shape appear on the tab

The GIMP can read many image file types – including PSD files produced by Photoshop.

4 Select the ✐ Paintbrush tool in the Toolbox and click on an image in the Image Window to paint star shapes

5 Now, select the ▦ Pattern tab and [Aa] Fonts tab in turn to examine the available items in those categories

6 The Layers, Channels and Paths panel has tabs that display items for each category. Each category provides a button to toggle the visibility of individual items. For example, select the ▦ Channels tab then click the 👁 eye button of the Red channel to hide all red components of the image

The results of some GIMP plugins can be less predictable than those in Photoshop for inexperienced users.

7 There are buttons at the bottom of the Layers, Channels and Paths panel that allow you to add, remove, or arrange items in each category. For example, select the ☰ Layers tab then click the 🗋 Create button to open a "Create a New Layer" dialog

8 Enter a layer name, such as "StarLayer", then click the **OK** button to close the dialog and see the new layer added in the Layers tab

Watching Movies

Linux Mint includes a fast, light-weight media player app named Celluloid that can play audio and video content in many file formats including AVI, MPG, WMV, WAV, MP3, and many more. Celluloid is the default media player for audio and video files in Linux Mint:

 Double-click on a video file icon to begin immediate playback of that video
or
Click **Menu**, **Sound & Video**, **Celluloid** to launch the media player app, then click **+**, **Open** and browse to a video file

Hot tip

The Celluloid media player also supports subtitles.

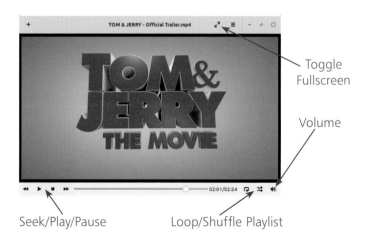

 Select a movie to see it immediately begin to play in the Celluloid app's display area

Toggle Fullscreen

Volume

Seek/Play/Pause

Loop/Shuffle Playlist

...cont'd

3 Click the **Volume** button and drag its pop-up slider to adjust the volume level

4 Drag the corner of the window to change its size – see border areas appear around the movie in the display area

You can advance a paused movie by dragging the slider, or by placing the cursor over the display area and rolling your mouse wheel.

5 Click the **Toggle Fullscreen** button to switch between a window and fullscreen views and see the video automatically resize

You can click the hamburger button and choose the **Toggle Controls** option to hide or show the controls.

Playing Music

The Rhythmbox music player is great for playing music files and is also a podcast aggregator – and an internet radio tuner:

1 Click **Menu**, **Sound & Video**, **Rhythmbox** to launch the Rhythmbox app

2 Select **Music** in the "Library" pane, then click the **Import** button on the toolbar

The ▶ Play button will change to a ❚❚ Pause button during playback.

3 Use the drop-down menu to choose a folder containing music files, such as a sub-folder within your **Music** folder

Right-click on a track and choose **Remove** to delete it from the playlist.

4 See Rhythmbox list the music files within the chosen folder as "tracks"

5 Click on the tracks in the list to select them, then click the **Import _n_ selected tracks** button to make a playlist

You can also right-click on a music file icon and choose **Open with**, **Rhythmbox** to play it.

6 Click the ▶ **Play** button to start playing from "Track 1" or double-click any listed track to play that track

...cont'd

7 Select **Radio** in the "Library" pane and double-click one of the listed radio stations to start listening

8 Select **Podcasts** in the "Library" pane, then click the **Add** button on the toolbar and search for podcasts by topic

9 Double-click on any podcast of interest to start listening

10 Click the **X** button to close the Rhythmbox window, then click the **Rhythmbox** icon on the System Tray and click the **X** button in the pop-up panel to exit the app

Hot tip

You can add more radio stations by clicking the **Add** button and entering a URL – use a search engine to find URLs for internet radio stations and podcasts.

Hot tip

A icon gets added to the System Tray when playback begins of music, podcasts or radio. You can close the Rhythmbox window and playback will continue. Click the icon and use the controls on the panel that appears to control playback, or click its **X** button to quit playback.

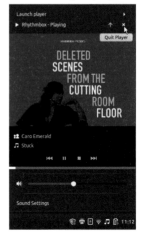

Streaming TV

Linux Mint includes a streaming app named "Hypnotix" that supports live TV, movies and series. The app does not provide content itself but streams content from IPTV (Internet Protocol TV) providers. Hypnotix is configured by default with only one IPTV provider called "Free-TV". This provider supplies only free, legal, publicly available content, and no adult content:

1 Click **Menu**, **Sound & Video**, **Hypnotix** to launch the Hypnotix app

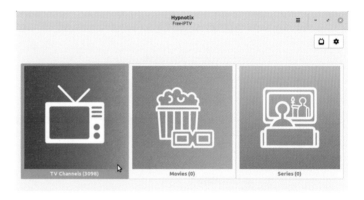

There are presently no Movies or Series, so those panels are inactive.

2 Click the **TV Channels** panel to see a selection of streaming services, listed with flags denoting their country of origin and the number of channels they offer

	Free-IPTV TV Channels	
GERMAN TV (34)	SAMSUNG TV PLUS (61)	Pluto Germany (88)
GERMAN Etc (4)	GERMAN LOCAL (57)	AUSTRIA (24)
SWITZERLAND (32)	SWITZERLAND MUSIK (4)	LIECHTENSTEIN (1)
USA (182)	USA MUSIK (6)	USA LOCAL (76)
USA GALXY TV (2)	DISTRO USA (33)	MYTVTOGO USA (25)
MYTVTOGO USA MUSIK (4)	PLEX USA (126)	PLUTO USA (282)
REDBOX USA (40)	ROKU USA (34)	STIRR USA (116)
STIRR USA MUSIK (2)	STIRR CITY USA (100)	TVS USA (29)
Bumblebee USA (47)	UDU TV USA (8)	AMC USA (5)
GINIKO USA (36)	CANADA (81)	GEM ONLINE (25)

Free-IPTV offers over 2000 legally available TV channels from all over the world.

3 Click on one of the listed services, such as "Redbox USA", to see a scrollable alphabetical list of channels appear alongside a display area

Hypnotix is a new app introduced in Linux Mint version 20.

4 Scroll through the list and click any channel to begin streaming its content to the display area

Your viewing experience depends on your connection speed.

5 Place your cursor over the display area, then use the pop-up controls to pause or resume live streaming TV

To add another IPTV provider, click the button on the launch screen, then click **Add a new provider** and enter the URL of an M3U playlist. Search online for "Free IPTV M3U Playlist".

Sharing Content

You can easily send files to another Linux PC on your local network using the Warpinator app. Each computer must be running the Warpinator app in order to be detected. Additionally, they must each use the same group code and port number, set in the Warpinator app's Preferences dialog window – by default, the group code is "Warpinator" and the port number is 42000.

 Select **Menu**, **Accessories**, **Warpinator** on a locally networked PC to see the app detect another Linux PC

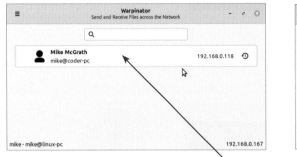

 Click on the other detected PC to which you want to send a file – to switch into a **File Transfers** window

 Next, browse to the file's location to select a file, or drag and drop the file onto the File Transfers window

The file will not be transferred until the user on the receiving PC gives their approval.

4 Now, click the **Send files** button – to send a request to the other PC

See a notification appear on the other PC describing the incoming file and requesting approval for the transfer

Warpinator is a new app introduced in Linux Mint version 20.

 The user on the other PC can click **Accept** to receive the file and the transfer will be made immediately to that PC

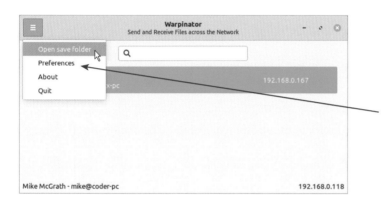

Select the **Preferences** item on this menu to choose file transfer options and configure the group code and port number if desired.

 Received files are automatically added to Warpinator's "save" folder on the other PC by default – click the ≡ hamburger button, then choose **Open save folder** to see all transferred files

Warpinator will continue running if you simply close the window. An icon is added to the System Tray that you can right-click and choose **Quit** to exit the app.

Summary

- The **Image Viewer** app displays images and can create a slideshow of multiple images.

- Image Viewer can make a selected image the Desktop background **wallpaper**.

- The **Pix** viewer app has a Browser mode and a Viewer mode.

- Pix viewer can arrange images and photos in a **Catalog** by grouping them with a common tag.

- The **Document Scanner** app can import images from a scanner.

- Scanned **text** and **photos** can be cropped and saved as a file.

- The GNU Image Manipulation Program (**GIMP**) is the primary image editing application in Linux.

- The GIMP app includes over 220 **plugins** that provide many of the capabilities of Adobe Photoshop.

- The **Celluloid** app can play audio and video content in many file formats.

- **Celluloid** app can play video in a window or fullscreen.

- **Rhythmbox** can import selected music files as **tracks** within a library.

- The Rhythmbox music player is also a podcast aggregator and an internet radio tuner.

- The **Hypnotix** app can stream live TV content.

- Hypnotix lists services supplied by Free-IPTV who only provide legally available channel content.

- The **Warpinator** app can transfer files to another Linux PC on your local network.

- To transfer files with Warpinator both PCs must be running Warpinator and the receiver must approve the transfer.

(8) Using Accessories

Writing Text

The plain text Text Editor app (**xed**) in Linux Mint is the equivalent of the Notepad app in Windows – but Text Editor has many more features. It can number lines, sort lines into alpha-numeric order, and it provides syntax highlighting for a whole range of scripting, programming, and markup languages.

You must recognize, however, that Linux does not treat text line endings in the same way as Windows. Linux adds a non-printing line feed **\n** ("newline") character, whereas Windows adds non-printing carriage return and line feed **\r\n** characters. This means that text files created in Linux do not maintain their line endings correctly when viewed on a Windows system. The Text Editor app provides an option when saving text files that lets you choose your preferred type of line endings:

The Notepad app in versions of the Windows 10 operating system from October 2018 supports both Linux LF (line feed) line endings, and Windows CRLF (carriage return + line feed) line endings.

126

1 Click **Menu**, **Accessories**, **Text Editor** to launch the app

2 Next, click **Tools**, **Autocheck Spelling** to turn the spellchecker on

3 Now, type in some lines of text – see the spellchecker place a red underline beneath any suspicious items

*Unsaved Document 1

File   Edit   View   Search   Tools   Documents   Help

*Unsaved Document 1

HTML in easy steps, 9th edition instructs you how to employ the latest development for web page design with HyperText Markup Language (HTML). Modern web browsers support exciting features of the HTML standard that allows easy creation of stunning web pages and engaging interactive apps.

Plain Text ▾   Spaces: 4 ▾   Ln 1, Col 288   INS

You can click **Edit**, **Sort lines** to rearrange the lines into alphanumeric order, then click **Edit**, **Undo** to revert to the original order.

4 Click **Edit**, **Preferences**, **Editor**, then slide the "Display line numbers" toggle switch to the "On" position – to see the lines get numbered

5 Click the **Close** button, click **Edit**, **Select All** (or press **Ctrl + A**) to select all text, then hit the **Delete** key to remove all text

6 Select **View**, **Highlight Mode**, **HTML** to turn on syntax highlighting for HTML markup code

7 Now, type in some HTML markup tags – see the elements, attributes and content appear colored

The line numbers appear only in the Text Editor window – they are not inserted into the text.

8 Click **File**, **Save As** to open a "Save As" dialog, then enter a file name and choose the **Windows** line ending option

9 Click the **Save** button, then copy the file to a Windows system and see the line endings are preserved

This file saved with Linux line endings may appear like this on older versions of Windows Notepad.

Doing Calculations

Linux Mint includes a Calculator app that can perform many different types of calculations and conversions. It provides a scrollable History View of your previous calculations so you can select a previous calculation to manipulate further.

There are five modes available in the Calculator app in which you can enter basic equations, execute math and financial functions, and perform conversions of currency, size, and number base:

 Click **Menu**, **Accessories**, **Calculator** to launch the app in "Basic Mode"

 Enter some equations to see the result and see them get added to the **History View** area

Hot tip

There is no limit to the number of calculations in the **History View** area.

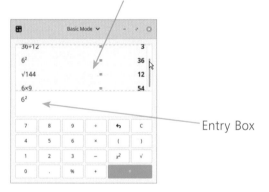

Entry Box

 Select "Advanced Mode" from the title bar menu, then select options to convert a measured distance

Don't forget

The **Advanced Mode** provides additional buttons that perform math functions, such as logarithm (**log**).

4 Select "Financial Mode" from the title bar menu, then select options to approximately convert a sum of currency

The **Financial Mode** provides additional buttons that perform financial functions such as future value (**Fv**).

5 Select "Programming Mode" from the title bar menu, then select options to convert number bases

Decimal 100 is binary **1100100**, which represents the sum of 64+32+0+0+4+0+0. Decimal 100 is also octal **144** and hexadecimal **64**.

The **Programming Mode** provides additional buttons that perform programming functions, such as Boolean algebra (**AND**, **OR**, **XOR**, **NOT**).

6 Select "Keyboard Mode" from the title bar menu, then select options to convert temperature scales

Managing Archives

The Linux Mint distro includes a versatile Archive Manager app that can compress files into many archive file formats. If you choose the popular ZIP (**.zip**) format you can password-protect the archive, but this format often does not produce the smallest archive file size. You can find the Archive Manager launcher on the Menu in the Accessories category, but usually you will launch it from a right-click context menu:

1 Right-click on a folder you would like to compress, and choose **Compress** on the context menu – to open a "Compress" dialog

2 Enter an archive file name, then select the **.zip** archive file format

Not all archive file formats support password protection.

The archive does not replace the original folder – it is created in addition to the original.

3 Choose a location and expand "Other Options", then enter a password

4 Click the **Create** button to make an archive copy of the original folder and its contents at your chosen location

5 Right-click on the original folder and choose **Delete** on the context menu – to remove the folder and its contents

...cont'd

6. Next, right-click on the archive file and choose **Open With Archive Manager** – to see its contents

7. Now, click the **Extract** button in an attempt to extract the folder and its contents

Hot tip

You can check an archive for errors by choosing the **Test Integrity** option on this menu.

Save As...
Password...
Test Integrity
Properties

8. Enter the password for this archive, then click the **OK** button – to extract a copy of the folder and its contents

Archive Manager

Password required for "Marques.zip"

Password:
●●●●●

Cancel   OK

Extraction completed successfully

Close   Show the Files

131

9. Click the **Close** button to exit the Archive Manager app

Hot tip

Click the **Show the Files** button to see the folder's contents listed in the Nemo file manager.

10. Create another archive of the same folder using the 7-ZIP (**.7z**) archive file format, and compare the file sizes

Hot tip

See page 168 for more on archive management.

Taking Notes

Linux Mint includes the Gnote app that lets you keep track of small pieces of information. You can use this in much the same way as Sticky Notes on Windows, but you can also add one or more links in a Gnote note to reference your other notes, and you can group Gnote notes by topic in notebooks:

1 Click **Menu**, **Accessories**, **Gnote** to launch the app

2 Click the button, then select **New Notebook** to open a dialog

3 Enter a name for the notebook, such as "Web", then click the **Create** button – see a "Web" notebook icon get added in the left-hand pane of the app

4 Select the new "Web" icon, then click the **+** button to create a new note that opens in a separate window

5 See that by default the new note contains a colored editable heading and a black editable paragraph

Hot tip

Gnote provides three default notebooks for **All** notes, **Important** notes, and **Unfiled** notes that have not been filed in any other notebook.

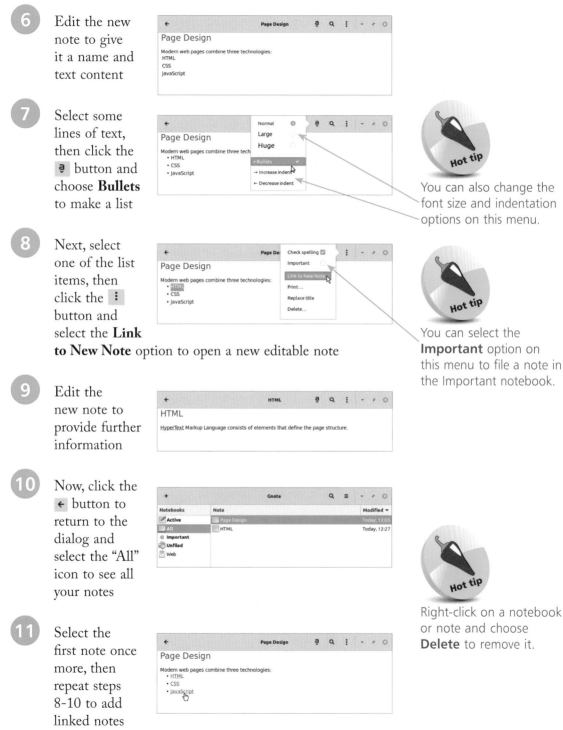

6 Edit the new note to give it a name and text content

7 Select some lines of text, then click the ੩ button and choose **Bullets** to make a list

Hot tip
You can also change the font size and indentation options on this menu.

8 Next, select one of the list items, then click the ⋮ button and select the **Link to New Note** option to open a new editable note

Hot tip
You can select the **Important** option on this menu to file a note in the Important notebook.

9 Edit the new note to provide further information

10 Now, click the ← button to return to the dialog and select the "All" icon to see all your notes

Hot tip
Right-click on a notebook or note and choose **Delete** to remove it.

11 Select the first note once more, then repeat steps 8-10 to add linked notes providing further information for the other list items

Grabbing Screenshots

As with the Windows operating system, in Linux Mint you can press the **Print Screen** button (**PrtSc**) to immediately capture an image of your screen or use the **Alt + PrtSc** key combination to immediately capture the currently-active window. Additionally, Linux Mint includes a Screenshot app that provides delay and other options – much like the Snipping Tool app in Windows:

1 Click **Menu**, **Accessories**, **Screenshot** to launch the app

2 Choose the "Grab the whole screen" option and select a delay period, then click the **Take Screenshot** button

3 Edit the Name and location, then click the **Save** button

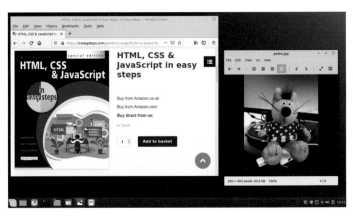

4 Relaunch the app, then choose the "Grab the current window" option

5 Select the "Include pointer" option, then click the **Take Screenshot** button

You can open the **Apply effect** drop-down menu to choose an effect when grabbing the current window.

6 Edit the name and location, then click the **Save** button

7 See that the screenshot includes the cursor and any pop-up tooltips

Window.png
197.3 kB

8 Relaunch the app, then choose the "Select area to grab" option, then click the **Take Screenshot** button

9 Drag the cursor to select a rectangular area of the screen, then release the mouse button to capture that area

You can also press **Shift** + **PrtSc** to see the cursor change to a crosshair so you can select an area of the screen to grab.

10 Edit the name and location, then click the **Save** button

Area.png
59.1 kB

Reading Documents

The Linux Mint distro includes the Document Viewer app (**xreader**) that is useful when reading multi-page documents such as a user guide. Typically, these types of documents are in the Portable Document Format (**.pdf**) that can contain annotations and are sometimes protected by a password. You can find the Document Viewer launcher on the Menu in the Accessories category, but usually you will launch it by double-clicking on a PDF document's file icon or from a right-click context menu:

1 Right-click on a document file icon and choose **Open With Document Viewer** to launch the app

2 If an "Enter password" dialog appears, enter the password then click the dialog's **Unlock Document** button – to see the first page of the document

Hot tip

If the Side Pane is not immediately visible, click **View**, **Side Pane** to make it appear.

Side Pane   Forward/Back   Zoom   View

Sorting Algorithms.pdf — Sorting Algorithms

File   Edit   View   Go   Bookmarks   Help

1   of 6

Thumbnails

Copying sorts

[0] [1] [2] [3] [4] [5]

| 5 | 3 | 1 | 2 | 6 | 4 |

1	2
1	2	3
1	2	3	4
1	2	3	4	5
1	2	3	4	5	6

Selecting sorts

...cont'd

3 Click the **Forward** button to advance the pages, or click on a "Thumbnail" in the Side Pane to jump to a page

4 Select the "Annotations" option in the Side Pane drop-down menu, then click on its icon to see the note

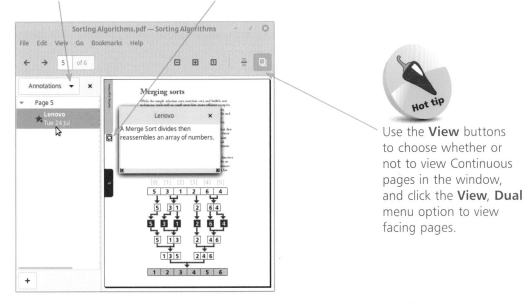

Hot tip

Use the **View** buttons to choose whether or not to view Continuous pages in the window, and click the **View**, **Dual** menu option to view facing pages.

5 Select the "Bookmarks" option in the Side Pane menu, then to mark a page, click **Bookmarks**, **Add Bookmark**

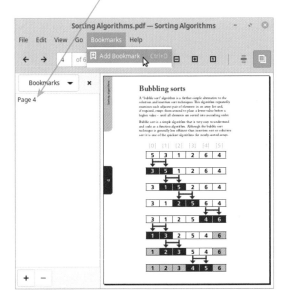

Hot tip

You can click **File**, **Properties** to discover a document's origin.

Summary

- The **Text Editor** app is a plain text editor that can number lines and sort lines alphanumerically.

- Text Editor can provide **syntax highlighting** for many scripting, programming, and markup languages.

- Linux does not treat text **line endings** in the same way as Windows, but Text Editor supports both types of endings.

- The **Calculator** app can perform basic equations, execute math and financial functions, and perform conversions.

- Calculator provides a scrollable **History View** of previous calculations so they can be quickly recalled.

- The **Archive Manager** app compresses files into many archive file formats.

- The **ZIP** file format supports password-protection but may not produce the smallest archive files.

- The **7-ZIP** file format produces smaller compressed archive files than the ZIP file format.

- The **Gnote** app can keep track of small pieces of information grouped in notebooks.

- **Gnote** supports **hyperlinks** to other notes.

- The **Screenshot** app can capture an image of the entire screen, current window, or a selected area.

- Screenshot provides **delay** and border options.

- The **Document Viewer** app can display multi-page documents and provide Thumbnail views of each page.

- Document Viewer supports **bookmarks** that mark a page for future reference.

- Document Viewer supports **annotations** that provide additional information on a page.

9 Commanding the Terminal

This chapter introduces the power of the command-line Terminal for file management and text manipulation.

Invoking the Terminal

At the very heart of the Linux operating system is a core series of machine instructions known as the "kernel" – this is a technical program that is not user-friendly, as it is mainly designed to communicate with electronic components. A Linux "shell" is a facility that allows the user to communicate via commands with the kernel in a human-readable form. It translates command-line instructions so they can be processed.

Most Linux distros include several shell programs that offer different features. The default Linux shell program, however, is called Bash (**B**ourne **A**gain **SH**ell), which is an updated version of the original Bourne shell found in the Unix operating system.

The shell understands a large number of commands, and each has a number of "options" that may (optionally) be specified to modify their behavior – usually these are prefixed by a hyphen. Many also accept "arguments" that provide data to be used by the command. The typical syntax of a shell command looks like this:

command -option argument

Shell commands can be executed at a prompt in a Terminal window on a graphical desktop interface:

 Click **Menu**, **Administration**, **Terminal** (or click the launcher on the Taskbar) to launch a Terminal window

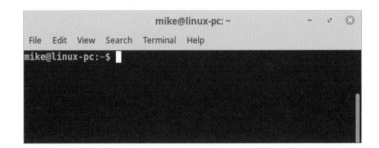

The Terminal window above displays the default **bash** command prompt and places the cursor after the prompt – ready to receive a command. The default prompt here comprises the current user name (**mike**), a separator character (@), the host PC name (**linux-pc**), the current directory (~ tilde character denoting the Home directory), and a final terminating character (**$**).

...cont'd

You can confirm the current user and host PC name at any time with the **whoami** and **hostname** commands:

 Type the **whoami** command at a prompt, then hit **Return**

 Now, type the **hostname** command and hit **Return** again

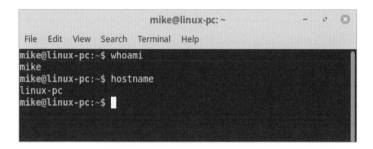

Commands use lowercase only – in uppercase the command will not be recognized.

Some commands call upon individual programs that reside on your system – for example, the **clear** command that removes previous content from the Terminal. Others are "builtin" commands that are built in to the shell itself – for example, the **exit** command that quits the shell and closes the Terminal window. You can determine whether a command is a builtin using the **type** command and the command's name as its argument:

 Type **clear** and hit **Return** to remove the previous content, then enter **type clear** and hit **Return** again to discover the location of the **clear** command program

5 Enter **type exit** and hit **Return** to discover that the **exit** command is a shell builtin instruction, then type the **exit** command and hit **Return** to quit the shell

Type a **--help** argument (two hyphens & "help") after any command, then hit **Return**, to see a list of options for that command.

Navigating at the Prompt

When you start a shell session you are, by default, located in your home directory of the Linux file system. You can switch to any directory to which you have access permission by stating its absolute address as the argument to the **cd** command. Similarly, you can return to your home directory by stating its absolute address as the argument to the **cd** command, or using its tilde alias with the command **cd ~**.

For shorter hierarchical moves, the command **cd ..** moves up one level to the parent directory of the current directory. Stating just the name of an immediate sub-directory as the argument to the **cd** command moves down one level to that sub-directory:

Beware

There must be space between the command and its argument.

 Launch a shell window then enter the **pwd** command at the prompt to print the current working directory

 Enter the combined command **cd /etc ; pwd** to switch to the **/etc** directory and confirm it as the working directory

 Next, enter the combined command **cd ~ ; pwd** to return to the home directory and confirm the location

 Enter the combined command **cd .. ; pwd** to switch to the parent directory and confirm the location

 Now, enter the combined command **cd mike ; pwd** to switch to the named sub-directory and confirm it

Don't forget

Replace **mike** with your own username in the combined command.

```
                              mike@linux-pc: ~            –   ⌄   ✕

File   Edit   View   Search   Terminal   Help

mike@linux-pc:~$ pwd
/home/mike
mike@linux-pc:~$ cd /etc ; pwd
/etc
mike@linux-pc:/etc$ cd ~ ; pwd
/home/mike
mike@linux-pc:~$ cd .. ; pwd
/home
mike@linux-pc:/home$ cd mike ; pwd
/home/mike
mike@linux-pc:~$ ▮
```

...cont'd

The contents of the current directory can be revealed using the **ls** command to display a list of its files and immediate sub-directories. This is a comprehensive command that has many useful options:

- Use the **-a** option to see all directory contents – including hidden files and hidden sub-directories.

- Use the **-l** option to see long format listing for each item – including user and group ownership names.

- Use the **-t** option to sort the contents by the time they were created or last modified.

- Use the **-o** option to suppress group ownership details.

- Use the **-g** option to suppress user ownership details.

Options can be combined to produce a complex option where each parameter is applied:

 Enter the command **cd "My Topics"** to move to an immediate sub-directory whose name contains a space

Next, enter the **ls** command to simply list all its contents

 Enter the command **ls -altog** to list all contents including hidden files, in long format, listed by modification time – but with user and group details suppressed

Directory names that contain spaces must be enclosed within quotation marks when specified as a command argument – to avoid truncation of the name.

143

```
mike@linux-pc: ~/My Topics           -  ⌀  ⊗

File  Edit  View  Search  Terminal  Help
mike@linux-pc:~$ cd "My Topics"
mike@linux-pc:~/My Topics$ ls
Articles   linux.txt   sample.txt
mike@linux-pc:~/My Topics$ ls -altog
total 20
drwxrwxr-x  3 4096 Jul 25 08:28 .
-rw-rw-r--  1 1137 Jul 25 08:28 linux.txt
-rw-rw-r--  1   31 Jul 25 08:26 sample.txt
drwxrwxr-x  2 4096 Jul 25 08:25 Articles
drwxr-xr-x 33 4096 Jul 25 08:25 ..
mike@linux-pc:~/My Topics$ █
```

All absolute directory addresses begin with a "/" character – as they descend from the / root location.

Operating on Directories

It is sometimes useful to be able to extract the name of a file, program or directory from the end of a path address using the **basename** command. Conversely, you can use the **dirname** command to remove the final part of the path address to a file – leaving just the path to its parent directory.

A new directory can be created in the current working directory by specifying a directory name of your choice as the argument to the **mkdir** command. Alternatively, a new directory can be created elsewhere by specifying a full path as the argument:

 To discover the location of the **bash** program that is the default shell, at a prompt enter the command **echo $SHELL**

 Issue a **basename $SHELL** command to extract the program name from the path address

 Issue a **dirname $SHELL** command to extract the parent directory of the **bash** program name from the path

 Enter the command **mkdir Sub1** to create a directory named "Sub1" in the current working directory

 Enter the command **mkdir /home/mike/Data/Sub2** to create a directory named "Sub2" using an absolute path address

The **basename** and **dirname** commands simply manipulate the path string – they do not implement any action.

```
mike@linux-pc: ~/Data

File  Edit  View  Search  Terminal  Help

mike@linux-pc:~/Data$ echo $SHELL
/bin/bash
mike@linux-pc:~/Data$ basename $SHELL
bash
mike@linux-pc:~/Data$ dirname $SHELL
/bin
mike@linux-pc:~/Data$ mkdir Sub1
mike@linux-pc:~/Data$ mkdir /home/mike/Data/Sub2
mike@linux-pc:~/Data$ pwd ; ls
/home/mike/Data
Sub1  Sub2
mike@linux-pc:~/Data$
```

Directories can be removed in the shell using the **rmdir** command. This takes the directory name as its argument and will instantly remove an empty directory, but will simply warn you that the directory is not empty if it contains files.

Having to delete files manually, one by one, may provide safeguards but can be tedious. An intelligent alternative is available by using the recursive interactive **-ri** option of the **rm** command. This steps inside the directory and examines every file – requesting your confirmation before deleting each file. When all files have been deleted it then asks if you want to delete the directory:

You can use a **-v** option with both the **rmdir** command and the **rm** command to produce verbose output – describing what is happening.

6 Launch the Text Editor using the **xed** command, and create three text files in the "Sub2" directory

7 Issue the command **rmdir Sub1** to remove the empty "Sub1" directory

8 Now, issue the command **rmdir Sub2** to attempt to remove the non-empty "Sub2" directory

9 Enter the command **rm -ri Sub2** to interactively delete the files within the "Sub2" directory, and remove the directory itself, by replying "Y" (yes) to each question

```
                        mike@linux-pc: ~/Data          –   ⌄  ⊗

File   Edit   View   Search   Terminal   Help
mike@linux-pc:~/Data$ ls
Sub1  Sub2
mike@linux-pc:~/Data$ rmdir Sub1
mike@linux-pc:~/Data$ rmdir Sub2
rmdir: failed to remove 'Sub2': Directory not empty
mike@linux-pc:~/Data$ rm -ri Sub2
rm: descend into directory 'Sub2'? Y
rm: remove regular file 'Sub2/file-2.txt'? Y
rm: remove regular file 'Sub2/file-1.txt'? Y
rm: remove regular file 'Sub2/file-3.txt'? Y
rm: remove directory 'Sub2'? Y
mike@linux-pc:~/Data$ ls
mike@linux-pc:~/Data$ ▮
```

If you're feeling brave, and are absolutely certain that the directory contains nothing you will miss, you can use the **rm** command with just a **-r** option to instantly delete a directory and its entire contents – use with care!

Managing Files

The shell **mv** command lets you easily move files around your Linux system from the command line. This command requires two arguments stating the name of the file to be moved, and the destination to which it should be moved. Interestingly, the **mv** command can also be used to rename a file by stating its current name and a new name as its two arguments.

If you wish to copy rather than move a file to a new location, the **cp** command can be used. This command can accept one or more files to be copied as its arguments, stating the destination as the final argument:

 Launch a shell Terminal window, then enter an **ls** command to see the contents of the current directory

 Issue an **mv** command to rename an existing file – for example, from "alpha.txt" to "zebra.txt" with **mv alpha. txt zebra.txt** – and an **ls** command to confirm the name change

 Enter **mv zebra.txt Box** to move the renamed file to a **Box** sub-directory – and an **ls** command to see it's gone

 Enter **cp some.txt Box** to copy a file named "some.txt" to the same sub-directory

Issue an **ls** command with the name of the sub-directory – confirming a file was moved and a file was copied

Hot tip

Use the **-i** option with the **mv** command to prompt before overwriting a file of the same name.

146

```
                          mike@linux-pc: ~/Data          –   ⌕   ⊗

   File   Edit   View   Search   Terminal   Help
   mike@linux-pc:~/Data$ ls
   alpha.txt  Box  some.txt
   mike@linux-pc:~/Data$ mv alpha.txt zebra.txt
   mike@linux-pc:~/Data$ ls
   Box  some.txt  zebra.txt
   mike@linux-pc:~/Data$ mv zebra.txt Box
   mike@linux-pc:~/Data$ ls
   Box  some.txt
   mike@linux-pc:~/Data$ cp some.txt Box
   mike@linux-pc:~/Data$ ls Box
   some.txt  zebra.txt
   mike@linux-pc:~/Data$ ▉
```

...cont'd

The **rm** command can be used to delete one or more files named as its arguments. The * wildcard can also be used to delete all files in a directory – if you are absolutely certain none are needed.

You can create hard links, pointing to the system address of a file, and soft (symbolic) links, storing the path to a file, with the **ln** command. By default, this will create a hard link to the file named as its argument – use its **-s** option to create a symbolic link.

The **readlink** command can be used to discover the target to which a symbolic link is pointing:

The wildcard * character means "all" and should be used with caution.

 Enter **rm Box/zebra.txt** to delete a file in a sub-directory and an **ls Box** command to confirm it's gone

 Enter **ln Box/some.txt hardlink** to create a hard link named "hardlink" to a file in the sub-directory

 Now, enter **ln -s Box/some.txt softlink** command to create a soft link named "softlink" to the same file

 Enter an **ls** command to see both links have been created in the home directory

Enter a **readlink softlink** command to see the target to which the soft link points

Hot tip

If you delete the target file a hard link will retain a copy of the file's content, but a soft link will simply point to a target that no longer exists.

147

```
mike@linux-pc: ~/Data                    –  ⌄  ⊗

File  Edit  View  Search  Terminal  Help
mike@linux-pc:~/Data$ ls
Box   some.txt
mike@linux-pc:~/Data$ rm Box/zebra.txt
mike@linux-pc:~/Data$ ls Box
some.txt
mike@linux-pc:~/Data$ ln Box/some.txt hardlink
mike@linux-pc:~/Data$ ln -s Box/some.txt softlink
mike@linux-pc:~/Data$ ls
Box   hardlink   softlink   some.txt
mike@linux-pc:~/Data$ readlink softlink
Box/some.txt
mike@linux-pc:~/Data$ █
```

Don't forget

You can find more details on shortcut links on page 68.

Examining File Properties

The Linux shell provides many commands that can be used to examine attributes of any file. The most comprehensive is the **stat** command that lists every important attribute of the file stated as its argument.

If you just want to discover the file size, use the **du** disk usage command with its **-b** option to count the number of bytes.

Use the **wc** word count command to quickly discover how many newlines, words, and bytes a text file contains, or assess what type of file it is with the **file** command:

Use the **wc** command with its **-m** option to just see a total word count.

 Enter **stat Box/some.txt** to discover the attributes of a file named "some.txt" in a **Box** sub-directory

 Enter **du -b Box/some.txt** to discover the size of this file in byte units

 Enter **wc Box/some.txt** to discover that file's line count, word count, and byte count

 Now, enter **file Box/some.txt** and **file Box/tux.png** commands to discover the file type of two files

See that here the **wc** command reveals the number of newlines (29), words (175), and bytes (1137) of this file.

```
                    mike@linux-pc: ~/Data           –   ⌄   ✕

File   Edit   View   Search   Terminal   Help
mike@linux-pc:~/Data$ stat Box/some.txt
  File: Box/some.txt
  Size: 1137           Blocks: 8            IO Block: 4096
Device: 802h/2050d     Inode: 21106964     Links: 1
Access: (0664/-rw-rw-r--)  Uid: ( 1000/    mike)
Access: 2023-07-25 08:59:15.859457000 +0300
Modify: 2023-07-25 08:28:31.476969000 +0300
Change: 2023-07-25 09:05:39.946732490 +0300
 Birth: -
mike@linux-pc:~/Data$ du -b Box/some.txt
1137    Box/some.txt
mike@linux-pc:~/Data$ wc Box/some.txt
  29  175 1137 Box/some.txt
mike@linux-pc:~/Data$ file Box/some.txt
Box/some.txt: UTF-8 Unicode text, with very long lines
mike@linux-pc:~/Data$ file Box/tux.png
Box/tux.png: PNG image data, 407 x 480, 8-bit/color RGBA, non
-interlaced
mike@linux-pc:~/Data$ █
```

The **touch** command introduces some interesting possibilities, as it can create an empty file and can change the Last Accessed and Last Modified timestamp attributes of a file. Used alone, it simply updates these to the present time, but used with a **-d** option it allows you to specify a date in a variety of formats – specify a day number and month number to set the timestamps to midnight on that day of the current year, or specify a complete date including year and time.

Date numbers supplied as an argument to the touch command must be enclosed within quotes.

5 Enter **touch -d "12/25" more.txt** to update the timestamps of a file named "more.txt" to a date in the current year

6 Enter a **stat more.txt** command to confirm the timestamps have been updated

7 Now, enter **touch -d \ "07/04/2023 12:00" more.txt** to update timestamps to the specified date, time, and year

8 Enter a **stat more.txt** command to confirm the timestamps have been updated once more

```
                          mike@linux-pc: ~/Data          –   ♦   ⊗
 File  Edit  View  Search  Terminal  Help
mike@linux-pc:~/Data$ touch -d "12/25" more.txt
mike@linux-pc:~/Data$ stat more.txt
  File: more.txt
  Size: 404          Blocks: 8          IO Block: 4096    r
Device: 802h/2050d   Inode: 1049166     Links: 1
Access: (0664/-rw-rw-r--)  Uid: ( 1000/    mike)  Gid: ( 100
Access: 2021-12-25 00:00:00.000000000 +0200
Modify: 2021-12-25 00:00:00.000000000 +0200
Change: 2021-03-09 14:28:17.173918815 +0200
 Birth: -
mike@linux-pc:~/Data$ touch -d \ "07/04/2023 12:00" more.txt
mike@linux-pc:~/Data$ stat more.txt
  File: more.txt
  Size: 404          Blocks: 8          IO Block: 4096    r
Device: 802h/2050d   Inode: 1049166     Links: 1
Access: (0664/-rw-rw-r--)  Uid: ( 1000/    mike)  Gid: ( 100
Access: 2023-07-04 12:00:00.000000000 +0300
Modify: 2023-07-04 12:00:00.000000000 +0300
Change: 2021-03-09 14:29:59.793902240 +0200
 Birth: -
mike@linux-pc:~/Data$ █
```

See that the properties indicate the date and time of the last change and the new timestamp after modification.

Comparing Files

The shell provides several ways to compare two files. You can check to see if two files are identical with the **cmp** command. If they are indeed identical, the command reports nothing, but if they differ, it reports the location of the first difference.

Text files can be compared line-by-line with the **comm** command. Its output is slightly unusual, as it creates three columns to indicate lines that match in each file:

- **Column 1** – lines found in the first file, but not the second.

- **Column 2** – lines found in the second file, but not the first.

- **Column 3** – lines found in both files.

1 Use a text editor to create a file named **abc.txt**, with three lines "Alpha", "Bravo", and "Charlie", and a file named **acd.txt** with three lines "Alpha", "Charlie" and "Delta" – save the files in the current directory

2 Launch a shell Terminal window and enter the command **cmp abc.txt acd.txt** to discover where the first difference occurs between these two files

3 Enter **comm abc.txt acd.txt** to see a line-by-line comparison

The **cmp** command can also be used to compare binary files such as images.

The **comm** command has options to suppress column output – the option **-12** suppresses the first two columns to show only lines that are common to both files.

```
                                    mike@linux-pc: ~/Data         -  ⌖  ⊗
  File  Edit  View  Search  Terminal  Help
mike@linux-pc:~/Data$ cmp abc.txt acd.txt
abc.txt acd.txt differ: byte 7, line 2
mike@linux-pc:~/Data$ comm abc.txt acd.txt
                    Alpha
Bravo
                    Charlie
        Delta
mike@linux-pc:~/Data$ 
```

...cont'd

The **diff** command offers an alternative to the **comm** command for comparison of text files. It too compares line-by-line, and it produces a detailed report showing any unique lines. It can also be used to compare two directories to reveal unique files.

Files may also be compared using checksum numbers to verify their integrity. Checksum numbers are often found on internet download pages so the user can ensure that a downloaded file is intact – typically, the checksum is made using the md5 algorithm.

The **md5sum** command produces a 32-byte checksum for the file specified as its argument, and should exactly match that stated by the originator if the file is indeed intact.

An alternative checksum can be created in much the same way by the **cksum** command. This generates a CRC (Cyclic Redundancy Check) value and includes the file's byte size in the output.

 Enter a **diff abc.txt acd.txt** command to discover those lines that are unique to each file

 Now, enter **md5sum abc.txt** to create a checksum number for that file

Similarly, enter **cksum abc.txt** to create another checksum number for that file

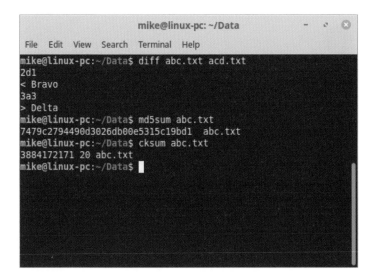

You can enter the command **man diff** to discover more about the diff output from its manual page.

Finding Files

Locating a file on your system can be achieved from a shell prompt using the **find** command. This is a very powerful command, with over 50 possible options, but it has an unusual syntax. Possibly the one most often used looks like this:

find *DirectoryName* **-type f -name** *FileName*

The directory name specifies the hierarchical starting point from which to begin searching. If you know the file exists somewhere in your home directory structure, you could begin searching there (~). The **-type f** option specifies that the search is for a file – denoted by the letter "f". The **-name** option makes the search by name – seeking the specified file name:

1 Enter **find ~ -type f -name some.txt** to seek all files named **some.txt** within your home directory structure

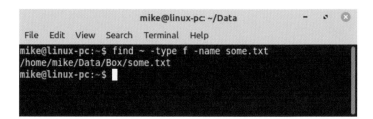

By default, the **find** command will only report the location of actual files, but you can also have it include symbolic links in the report by adding a **-L** option as its very first argument:

2 Now, enter **find -L ~ -type f -name some.txt** to see the result now locate the file and a symbolic link to that file – and an error message!

```
mike@linux-pc: ~/Data                   –   ·  ⊗
File  Edit  View  Search  Terminal  Help
mike@linux-pc:~$ find -L  ~  -type f -name some.txt
/home/mike/Data/some.txt
/home/mike/Data/Box/some.txt
find: File system loop detected; '/home/mike/.local/share/web
kitgtk/databases/indexeddb/v0' is part of the same file syste
m loop as '/home/mike/.local/share/webkitgtk/databases/indexe
ddb'.
mike@linux-pc:~$ █
```

Hot tip

Use the wildcard * with the file name when you know the name but not the extension.

Don't forget

You can recall the last command entered by pressing the **Up** arrow key.

...cont'd

If a search result includes error messages, you can exclude error messages by appending **2>/dev/null** to the command:

3 Enter **find -L ~ \ -type f -name some.txt 2>/dev/null** to seek the location of a file, report the location of any softlinks to that file, and suppress error messages

Hot tip

The \ backslash in this command simply lets you continue the command on the next line. Hit **Enter** after you type the \ backslash to see a continuation prompt appear on the next line.

In addition to searching for files, the **-type** option can specify that the search is for directories – denoted by the letter "d".

When searching deep directory structures, with many sub-directory levels, it is sometimes desirable to limit the depth of search with the **find** command's **-maxdepth** option. This requires an integer argument to specify the number of levels to search:

4 Enter **find /usr -maxdepth 1 -type d** to report only those directories that are direct descendants of the **/usr** directory

Hot tip

The **/usr** directory has many levels – remove the **-maxdepth 1** option from the command in Step 4 and run the command again to see all directories.

Reading Text Files

The simplest way to view a text file in the shell is with the **cat** command. Just state one or more files to view as its arguments and it will display their content, concatenating the text together. Viewing one or two small text files will fit comfortably in a single window so you will see the entire text. Larger files, however, will exceed the space in a single window so you will only see the final part of the text. The solution is to send the text stream to the **less** command via the "|" pipe operator. This means that the text is displayed one screen at a time, starting from the beginning:

 At a shell prompt, enter **cat quote1.txt quote2.txt** to display the content of two text files on standard output

You can use a **-n** option with the **cat** command to number each line on standard output.

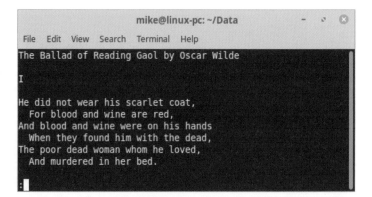

 Now, type **cat ballad.txt | less** then hit **Return** to display the file contents in **less** mode – in which a ":" prompt appears below the content text where you can enter special **less** mode commands to display selective text

The "less" facility offers many great options – press the **H** key in less mode to see them all.

Use the **Page Up** and **Page Down** keys to scroll through the text in **less** mode, then press the > key to skip to the end of the text and hit the Q key to quit **less** mode

The **head** command lets you preview the first 10 lines of a text file, and its companion **tail** command lets you preview the final 10 lines – great for skipping to the end of a long log file.

You can also display text with added line numbers using the **nl** number line command that provides useful control over numbering. Its **-v** option specifies an integer at which to start numbering, and its **-b t** option numbers only non-empty lines.

4. Enter the command **tail ballad.txt** to preview the last 10 lines of text within the file (including empty lines)

5. Now, enter **nl -v 0 -b t ballad.txt | head** to preview the first 10 lines of text – numbered starting at zero, and numbering only non-empty lines

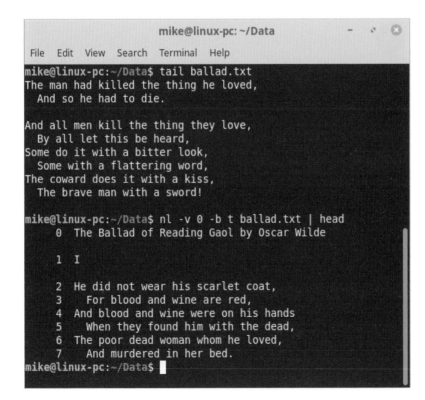

```
mike@linux-pc: ~/Data

File  Edit  View  Search  Terminal  Help
mike@linux-pc:~/Data$ tail ballad.txt
The man had killed the thing he loved,
  And so he had to die.

And all men kill the thing they love,
  By all let this be heard,
Some do it with a bitter look,
  Some with a flattering word,
The coward does it with a kiss,
  The brave man with a sword!

mike@linux-pc:~/Data$ nl -v 0 -b t ballad.txt | head
     0  The Ballad of Reading Gaol by Oscar Wilde

     1  I

     2  He did not wear his scarlet coat,
     3    For blood and wine are red,
     4  And blood and wine were on his hands
     5    When they found him with the dead,
     6  The poor dead woman whom he loved,
     7    And murdered in her bed.
mike@linux-pc:~/Data$ ▮
```

Don't forget

The shell pipeline technique allows the output from any command to be redirected as input for another command.

Writing Text Files

The classic Linux shell program for creating and editing text files is the compact **vi** application that is also found on Unix systems:

1 Type **vi** at a shell prompt, then hit **Return** to open the text editor in the shell window at its "splash screen"

```
                    mike@linux-pc: ~/Data          -    ⌄   ⊗
File   Edit   View   Search   Terminal   Help

                     VIM - Vi IMproved

        type  :q<Enter>               to exit
        type  :help<Enter>   or  <F1>   for on-line help
        type  :help version8<Enter>    for version info
```

The **vi** (vim) editor displays a tilde character at the beginning of each empty line. You cannot enter any text initially, as **vi** opens in "command mode" where it will attempt to interpret anything you type as an instruction:

2 Press the **Insert** key to change to "insert mode" where text can be input

3 In insert mode, type some text into the **vi** editor – the splash screen information disappears as you begin typing

```
                    mike@linux-pc: ~/Data          -    ⌄   ⊗
File   Edit   View   Search   Terminal   Help
This is some simple text that is being written using
the Vi text editor in a Linux shell.█
```

In command mode you can enter a **dd** command to delete the line where the cursor is currently positioned.

156

4 To save your text as a file, first hit the **Esc** key to exit "insert mode", switching **vi** to "command mode"

...cont'd

5 Type a ":" colon to begin a **vi** command – a colon character appears at the bottom-left corner of the editor

6 Now, type a lowercase "w" (for "write") followed by a space and a name for the text file – **simple.txt**, for example

7 Hit the **Return** key to write the file – in the current directory by default

8 Type a ":q" **vi** command then hit **Return** to close **vi** and return to a regular shell prompt

Using **vi** needs a little practice. Some distros, such as Linux Mint and Ubuntu, ship with other text editors – try typing "nano" at a prompt to launch an alternative text editor app.

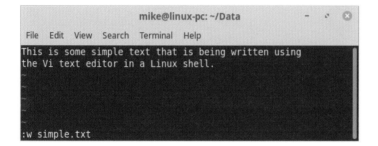

```
                    mike@linux-pc: ~/Data          -  °  ✕
   File  Edit  View  Search  Terminal  Help
  This is some simple text that is being written using
  the Vi text editor in a Linux shell.
  ~
  ~
  ~
  ~
  ~
  :w simple.txt
```

You can launch **vi** and open a file for editing in one single action by typing **vi** at a prompt, followed by a space and the file name:

9 At a shell prompt, enter the command **vi simple.txt** to re-open the text file in the **vi** editor

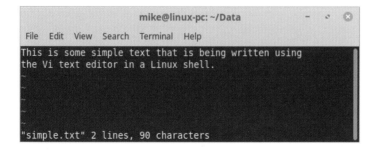

```
                    mike@linux-pc: ~/Data          -  °  ✕
   File  Edit  View  Search  Terminal  Help
  This is some simple text that is being written using
  the Vi text editor in a Linux shell.
  ~
  ~
  ~
  ~
  ~
  "simple.txt" 2 lines, 90 characters
```

To edit a file opened in **vi** you need to first hit the **Insert** key to enter insert mode.

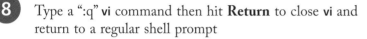

Manipulating Text Content

The shell **cut** and **paste** commands may not be what you expect. They work with text arranged in columns, delimited by an invisible tab character. Each column of text is known as a "field" and the **cut** command can specify which field to display – for instance, the option **-f3** chooses the third column from the left. The **paste** command is the opposite of the **cut** command, combining columns from multiple files for display horizontally:

Don't forget

Multiple fields can be specified as a comma-separated list, like **-f1,3** or as a range such as **-f2-4**.

 Use **vi** to create two text files "nums.txt" and "vegs.txt", each with two columns of text separated by tab characters

 Enter **cat nums.txt vegs.txt** to display the file contents vertically, one above the other

 Now, enter **paste nums.txt vegs.txt** to display the file contents horizontally, side-by-side

 Enter **cut -f2 vegs.txt** to just display the contents from the second column of one file

```
                          mike@linux-pc: ~/Data        -  *  x

 File  Edit  View  Search  Terminal  Help
mike@linux-pc:~/Data$ cat nums.txt vegs.txt
One     Four
Two     Five
Three   Six
Tomato  Cucumber
Lettuce Onion
Cabbage Cauliflower
mike@linux-pc:~/Data$ paste nums.txt vegs.txt
One     Four    Tomato  Cucumber
Two     Five    Lettuce Onion
Three   Six     Cabbage Cauliflower
mike@linux-pc:~/Data$ cut -f2 vegs.txt
Cucumber
Onion
Cauliflower
mike@linux-pc:~/Data$
```

Simple text transformations can easily be made by piping a text stream to the **tr** command. This requires two arguments to specify what to change, and how it should be changed. For instance, the command **tr a "*"** changes all occurrences of the letter "a", replacing each one with an asterisk on standard output.

Typically, the **tr** command is used to transform capitalization on output. The **sort** command is often used at the end of a pipeline to display lines of text sorted alphabetically. It can also be used to order lines numerically if a **-n** option is used. The **tee** command is useful in a pipeline that ends with a **sort** instruction to write the text stream as a file before sorting. The file name is specified by the argument to the **tee** command and the file is created in the current directory:

 Enter **cat quote3.txt ; \ cat quote3.txt | tr "a-z" "A-Z"** to display the contents of a file named "quote1.txt" – both in its original format and after transformation to uppercase

Beware

Remember that the sequence of characters specified to the **tr** command must be enclosed in quotes.

6 Enter **cut -f2 vegs.txt | sort** to just display the contents of a second column, sorted alphabetically

7 Now, enter **cut -f2 vegs.txt \ | tee vegs-column2.txt | sort** to save a second column as a text file before displaying it sorted alphabetically on standard output

8 Finally, enter **cat vegs-column2.txt** to display the file

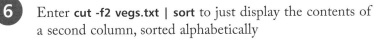

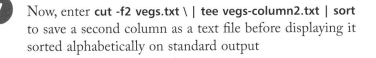

```
mike@linux-pc: ~/Data
File  Edit  View  Search  Terminal  Help
mike@linux-pc:~/Data$ cat quote3.txt ; \
> cat quote3.txt | tr "a-z" "A-Z"
I can resist everything except temptation.

I CAN RESIST EVERYTHING EXCEPT TEMPTATION.

mike@linux-pc:~/Data$ cut -f2 vegs.txt | sort
Cauliflower
Cucumber
Onion
mike@linux-pc:~/Data$ cut -f2 vegs.txt \
> | tee vegs-column2.txt | sort
Cauliflower
Cucumber
Onion
mike@linux-pc:~/Data$ cat vegs-column2.txt
Cucumber
Onion
Cauliflower
mike@linux-pc:~/Data$
```

Hot tip

Use a **-a** option with the **tee** command to append text to a file, rather than overwriting previous text.

Matching Text Patterns

The **grep** command is one of the most useful of all commands. It has many possible options, but its purpose is simply to display all lines from a text file that contain a specified string or pattern. A **grep** command can specify a string to seek as its first argument, and a file name in which to search as its second argument:

1 At a shell prompt, enter **grep sword ballad.txt** to display all lines in this text file that contain the word "sword"

```
                    mike@linux-pc: ~/Data         –  ⌀  ⊗
    File  Edit  View  Search  Terminal  Help
mike@linux-pc:~/Data$ grep sword ballad.txt
   The brave man with a sword!
For, right within, the sword of Sin
   The brave man with a sword!
mike@linux-pc:~/Data$
```

Hot tip

The **grep** command can also match regular expressions. For instance, **grep [Y] ballad.txt** would output all lines that have an uppercase Y. See the **grep** man page for more on regular expressions.

Notice that the output above has two duplicate lines. The **sort** command can be used to reorder lines – to make duplicate lines appear in succession – and duplicated successive lines can be removed with the **uniq** command. Output from the **grep** command can be piped to a **sort** command to make the duplicate lines successive, then piped to **uniq** so only unique lines remain:

2 Enter **grep sword ballad.txt \ | sort | uniq** to display all unique lines in this text file that contain the word "sword"

```
                    mike@linux-pc: ~/Data         –  ⌀  ⊗
    File  Edit  View  Search  Terminal  Help
mike@linux-pc:~/Data$ grep sword ballad.txt \
> | sort | uniq
For, right within, the sword of Sin
   The brave man with a sword!
mike@linux-pc:~/Data$
```

The **look** command is useful to quickly output all lines of text from a file that begin with a specified prefix. It can accept a **-d** option to only seek to match alphanumeric characters.

...cont'd

 3 Enter **look -d Y ballad.txt** to see a list of lines beginning with the letter "Y" from this file, ignoring spaces and tabs

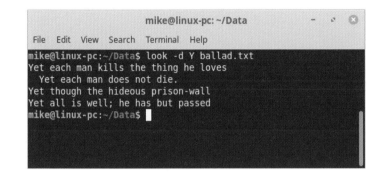

```
                        mike@linux-pc: ~/Data          -  ·  ⊗
  File  Edit  View  Search  Terminal  Help
mike@linux-pc:~/Data$ look -d Y ballad.txt
Yet each man kills the thing he loves
  Yet each man does not die.
Yet though the hideous prison-wall
Yet all is well; he has but passed
mike@linux-pc:~/Data$ █
```

Hot tip

You can also use the **look** command with a string argument to see a list of words starting with that string – taken from an editable dictionary file that is normally located at **/usr/share/dict/words**.

The **aspell** program is a powerful spellchecker that has a **-c** option that lets you interactively check a file for spelling errors. This highlights possible errors and suggests alternatives that you can choose to replace or ignore each highlighted word in turn:

4 Enter **aspell -c ballad.txt** to begin the spellchecker for this text file

5 Type the number against a suggested replacement to immediately replace the highlighted word with it

```
                        mike@linux-pc: ~/Data          -  ·  ⊗
  File  Edit  View  Search  Terminal  Help
And the sky above my head became
  Like a casque of scorching steel;
And, though I was a soul in pain,
  My pain I could not feel.

1) Basque            6) case
2) basque            7) Cassie
3) masque            8) cask
4) claque            9) caste
5) Case              0) cirque
i) Ignore            I) Ignore all
r) Replace           R) Replace all
a) Add               l) Add Lower
b) Abort             x) Exit

?
```

Don't forget

Press the **I** key to ignore a word, the **R** key to type your own replacement, or the **X** key to exit the **aspell** spellchecker.

Summary

- The **whoami** command reveals the user name, **hostname** reveals the host PC name, **clear** empties the shell window, and **exit** terminates the shell session.

- The **pwd** command reveals the current working directory and the directory location can be changed with the **cd** command.

- The ~ tilde character is an alias for the home directory and any directory's content can be revealed by the **ls** command.

- The **basename** command returns the last part of an address, whereas the **dirname** command returns just the first part.

- New directories are created with the **mkdir** command, and empty directories can be removed by the **rmdir** command.

- Files are moved or renamed with the **mv** command, copied with the **cp** command, and removed with the **rm** command.

- The **ln** command is used to create hard links and soft links, but the **readlink** command can only be used with soft links.

- The **stat** command lists all file properties, **du** reports the file size, and the **file** command reports the file type.

- Timestamps of a file can be modified by the **touch** command, and the **wc** command can be used to report the word count.

- Files can be compared with **cmp, comm,** and **diff** commands, and checksums generated by the **cksum** and **md5** commands.

- The **find** command locates a file, **grep** locates a string within a file, and **look** locates lines beginning with a given letter.

- Files can be viewed using the **cat** command, lines numbered with **nl**, and spelling checked by the **aspell** command.

- The **head** command displays the first 10 lines of a file, whereas the **tail** command displays its final 10 lines.

- The **vi** editor can be used to create text files and individual text columns manipulated by the **cut** and **paste** commands.

- A shell pipeline directs output to be used as input for another command and can include **tee** to write a file, **tr** to transform the output, and **sort** to order the output alphanumerically.

10 Performing Operations

Becoming the Superuser

A regular user can call upon many shell commands, but some are only available to a privileged "superuser". These restricted commands typically perform system administration functions to which regular users should not be allowed instant access.

On a typical home Linux system, the default user created during installation is given access to the **sudo** command, which allows commands to be executed as if the regular user is the superuser.

The **sudo** command is most often needed where you receive a "Permission denied" message when attempting to perform an operation. Prefixing the previous command with the **sudo** command effectively grants the required permission. If the previous command was lengthy, you can simply issue a **sudo !!** command to run it again with the required **sudo** prefix:

 At a shell prompt, enter **parted /dev/sda** to attempt to launch the partition editor for the hard-drive device

 As the shell informs you that you are not the superuser, type **c** then hit **Return** to cancel the attempt

Storage devices ("sd") on your system are labeled alphabetically, so the first device on your system is labeled **sda**.

```
                         mike@linux-pc: ~                    _   *   ⊗

  File   Edit   View   Search   Terminal   Help
mike@linux-pc:~$ parted /dev/sda
WARNING: You are not superuser.   Watch out for permissions.
Error: Error opening /dev/sda: Permission denied


Retry/Cancel? c
mike@linux-pc:~$ █
```

 Now, enter **sudo parted /dev/sda** (or just enter **sudo !!**) to launch the partition editor successfully

 At the **(parted)** prompt, enter a **print** command to list the partition information for the hard drive

 Now, enter a **help** command to see the available operations that may be performed, or enter a **quit** command to exit the partition editor

```
                        mike@linux-pc: ~           -   ⌄   ⊗
 File  Edit  View  Search  Terminal  Help
mike@linux-pc:~$ sudo parted /dev/sda
[sudo] password for mike:
GNU Parted 3.2
Using /dev/sda
Welcome to GNU Parted! Type 'help' to view a list of commands
(parted) print
Model: ATA ST500LT012-1DG14 (scsi)
Disk /dev/sda: 500GB
Sector size (logical/physical): 512B/4096B
Partition Table: gpt
Disk Flags:

Number  Start    End     Size    File system  Name
     Flags
 1      1049kB   538MB   537MB   fat32        EFI System
                                              Partition  boot
 2      538MB    500GB   500GB   ext4
(parted) quit
mike@linux-pc:~$ ▉
```

The root superuser can access any file or program on the system – with the potential to wreak havoc! Only log in as the root superuser if it's absolutely essential.

To assume superuser status in order to perform system administration, the **sudo** command can be used together with the **su** (switch user) command. This makes you the "root" user, with system-wide access, whose home directory is the **/root** directory:

 6   Issue the **sudo su** command, then enter your regular user password to assume superuser status

7   Enter **cd ~ ; pwd** to navigate to the root superuser's home directory and display its location

8   Log out from the root superuser account by entering the **exit** command – to resume regular user status back in the user's home directory

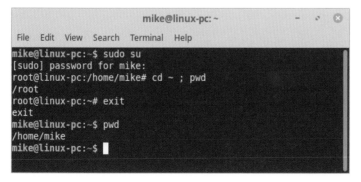

```
                        mike@linux-pc: ~           -   ⌄   ⊗
 File  Edit  View  Search  Terminal  Help
mike@linux-pc:~$ sudo su
[sudo] password for mike:
root@linux-pc:/home/mike# cd ~ ; pwd
/root
root@linux-pc:~# exit
exit
mike@linux-pc:~$ pwd
/home/mike
mike@linux-pc:~$ ▉
```

For security, the shell displays no characters for password entries.

165

Installing Packages

The Advanced Packaging Tool (APT) is a command-line tool that automates the process of retrieving, configuring, and installing software packages. It relies upon online repositories to locate software and resolve dependencies – so that the installation package will include any libraries required by the application. Unsurprisingly, as package installation modifies your system, all APT commands must be run using **sudo** for superuser privileges.

The APT's **apt-get** command has several options with which to manage packages. It's useful to first execute an **apt-get update** command to update the list of available repository packages, before issuing an **apt-get install** *package-name* command.

Once installed, a package can be upgraded to the latest version with an **apt-get upgrade** *package-name* command.

Use **apt-cache search** *package-name* to locate an installed or available package.

166

After a package has been installed it can be removed later using an **apt-get remove** *package-name* command – but this retains the configuration files for that package. For complete removal of a package and its configuration files, you can instead use the command **apt-get --purge remove** *package-name*.

 1 Enter the **sudo apt-get update** command to ensure the package list is up-to-date

2 Now, issue a command to install a package – for example, enter **sudo apt-get install gnome-mahjongg** (note **gg** ending) to install a graphical tiles game package

Use **man apt-get** to see the full range of options.

```
                          mike@linux-pc: ~              -  ○  ✕
 File   Edit   View   Search   Terminal   Help
mike@linux-pc:~$ sudo apt-get install gnome-mahjongg
Reading package lists... Done
Building dependency tree
Reading state information... Done
The following NEW packages will be installed:
  gnome-mahjongg
```

3 Some packages request confirmation before installation that requires you to type **Y** and hit Return if you are happy to proceed, or enter **N** to cancel the installation

```
Fetched 2520 kB in 2s (1618 kB/s)
Selecting previously unselected package gnome-mahjongg.
(Reading database ... 355137 files and directories currently installed.)
Preparing to unpack .../gnome-mahjongg_1%3a3.36.1-1_amd64.deb ...
Unpacking gnome-mahjongg (1:3.36.1-1) ...
Setting up gnome-mahjongg (1:3.36.1-1) ...
Processing triggers for desktop-file-utils (0.24+linuxmint1) ...
Processing triggers for mime-support (3.64ubuntu1) ...
Processing triggers for hicolor-icon-theme (0.17-2) ...
Processing triggers for gnome-menus (3.36.0-1ubuntu1) ...
Processing triggers for libglib2.0-0:amd64 (2.64.6-1~ubuntu20.04.1) ...
Processing triggers for man-db (2.9.1-1) ...
mike@linux-pc:~$
```

After the packages are retrieved, unpacked and set up, the installation is complete and the application is ready to run:

④ Check the Menu to see that a new Games category containing a launch icon has been added for the newly-installed package – click **Games**, **Mahjongg** to play

The Synaptic Package Manager is a user-friendly graphical interface for the Advanced Packaging Tool (APT) – in Linux Mint, click **Menu**, **Administration**, **Synaptic Package Manager** to launch the app.

Handling Archives

The traditional file compression tool in Linux uses the **gzip** command to compact one or more files into a single archive – adding a ".gz" file extension and replacing the original files. Its companion **gunzip** command can be used to extract files from an archive created with **gzip** – replacing the compressed archive:

1 Enter **du -b ele*** to learn the byte size of local files whose names begin "ele" – in this case, it's one named **elegy.txt**

2 Next, enter **gzip elegy.txt** to create a compressed archive of that file – named with an added ".gz" file extension

3 Now, use a further **du -b ele*** command to compare the file size of the compressed **gzip** archive to the original file

4 Enter **gunzip elegy.txt.gz** to extract the original file

```
                         mike@linux-pc: ~/Data          -   ⌄   ✕

 File   Edit   View   Search   Terminal   Help
mike@linux-pc:~/Data$ du -b ele*
6239    elegy.txt
mike@linux-pc:~/Data$ gzip elegy.txt
mike@linux-pc:~/Data$ du -b ele*
3051    elegy.txt.gz
mike@linux-pc:~/Data$ gunzip elegy.txt.gz
mike@linux-pc:~/Data$
```

Don't forget

A **bzip2** archive file size is smaller than gzip and zip archives – notice the size of the archives in these examples.

The modern **bzip2** compression tool gets better compression than **gzip** but is less widely used – distributing **bzip2** archives may not find universal acceptance. It works like the **gzip** tool, but adds a ".bz2" file extension and has a companion **bunzip2** uncompressor:

5 Enter **du -b ele*** to learn the byte size of local files whose names begin "ele" – in this case, it's one named **elegy.txt**

6 Next, enter **bzip2 elegy.txt** to create a compressed archive of that file – named with an added ".bz2" file extension

7 Now, use a further **du -b ele*** command to compare the file size of the compressed **bzip2** archive to the original file

8 Enter **bunzip2 elegy.txt.bz2** to extract the original file – being sure to include the added ".bz2" file extension

```
                     mike@linux-pc: ~/Data
 File   Edit   View   Search   Terminal   Help
mike@linux-pc:~/Data$ du -b ele*
6239    elegy.txt
mike@linux-pc:~/Data$ bzip2 elegy.txt
mike@linux-pc:~/Data$ du -b ele*
2768    elegy.txt.bz2
mike@linux-pc:~/Data$ bunzip2 elegy.txt.bz2
mike@linux-pc:~/Data$
```

Compressed archives created in Windows systems invariably use the zip compression format. In Linux systems their contents can be extracted by the **unzip** command and archives created for distribution to Windows users with the **zip** command. The **unzip** command does not delete the archive file after extraction:

9 Enter **zip elegy.zip elegy.txt** to specify the archive name and the file it should contain in compressed form

10 Issue another **du -b ele*** command to compare file sizes, then enter **unzip elegy.zip** to extract the archive contents

11 When asked, choose the "r" option, then rename the extracted file **elegy.unzipped** – to differ from the original

```
                     mike@linux-pc: ~/Data
 File   Edit   View   Search   Terminal   Help
mike@linux-pc:~/Data$ zip elegy.zip elegy.txt
  adding: elegy.txt (deflated 52%)
mike@linux-pc:~/Data$ du -b ele*
6239    elegy.txt
3191    elegy.zip
mike@linux-pc:~/Data$ unzip elegy.zip
Archive:  elegy.zip
replace elegy.txt? [y]es, [n]o, [A]ll, [N]one, [r]ename: r
new name: elegy.unzipped
  inflating: elegy.unzipped
mike@linux-pc:~/Data$
```

Beware

The **zip** command requires the archive name as its first argument, followed by a list of files to be included in that archive.

169

Hot tip

Use a **-c** option with **gunzip**, **bunzip2**, or **unzip** commands to display the content of compressed text files on standard output.

Examining File Systems

A Linux system may span multiple hard disk drives and extend across many disk partitions. Each partition is represented by a special file in the **/dev** directory – typically, **/dev/sda1** may represent the first partition on your master hard disk drive. During installation of the Linux operating system, each partition is formatted as a persistent storage "file system" on the hard drive in which files can be stored and recalled. Similarly, media drives are formatted with their own file systems in which to store data. Media drives must be "mounted" onto the Linux file tree in order to make them accessible, and this can be achieved automatically:

 Click **Menu, Accessories, Files** – to open the "Nemo" file manager

 In Nemo, click **Edit, Preferences, Behavior**, then scroll down to the "Media Handling" category

	File Management Preferences				
Views	Behavior	Display	List Columns	Preview	Toolbar

Media Handling

☑ Automatically mount removable media when inserted and on startup
☑ Automatically open a folder for automounted media
☐ Prompt or autorun/autostart programs when media are inserted
☐ Automatically close the device's tab, pane, or window when a device is unmounted or ejected

Close

 Now, ensure that the option to "Automatically mount removable media when inserted and on startup" is selected

 Click the **Close** button to confirm the selection and to close the "File Management Preferences" dialog

The **df** disk free command shows how file systems are being used by indicating free space. It has a **-h** option to make the output more understandable and a **-T** option to display file system types:

 Insert a flash drive into a USB port on your device

 Open a **Terminal** window, then enter the command **df -hT** to discover how the file system currently appears

Beware

The **df -T** option (uppercase) will display file system types, whereas the **df -t** option (lowercase) specifies which file system types to list.

```
                          mike@linux-pc: ~          -  ×  ⊗

  File  Edit  View  Search  Terminal  Help
  mike@linux-pc:~$ df -hT
  Filesystem      Type      Size  Used  Avail  Use%  Mounted on
  udev            devtmpfs  1.9G     0   1.9G    0%  /dev
  tmpfs           tmpfs     384M  1.3M   382M    1%  /run
  /dev/sda2       ext4      457G   23G   412G    6%  /
  tmpfs           tmpfs     1.9G   24M   1.9G    2%  /dev/shm
  tmpfs           tmpfs     5.0M  4.0K   5.0M    1%  /run/lock
  tmpfs           tmpfs     1.9G     0   1.9G    0%  /sys/fs/cgroup
  /dev/sda1       vfat      511M  4.7M   507M    1%  /boot/efi
  tmpfs           tmpfs     384M   44K   384M    1%  /run/user/1000
  /dev/sdb1       vfat      3.9G   44K   3.9G    1%  /media/mike/USB DRIVE
  mike@linux-pc:~$ █
```

Here, the hard drive file systems on **/dev/sda1** and **/dev/sda2**
were automatically mounted onto the Linux file tree during the
boot process, and the media drive file system on **/dev/sdb1** was
automatically mounted when the flash drive was inserted into the
device port. A file system can be manually unmounted using the
umount command to perform maintenance on it without fear of
file corruption. For instance, the root superuser can run the **fsck**
file system check command to check for integrity and errors:

7 Enter **umount /dev/sdb1** to unmount the file system on
the USB flash drive

8 Now, issue the command **sudo fsck /dev/sdb1** to check the
USB flash drive file system for errors

9 When the check completes, remove the flash drive from
the USB port – reinsert it into the port to mount it again

```
                          mike@linux-pc: ~          -  ×  ⊗

  File  Edit  View  Search  Terminal  Help
  mike@linux-pc:~$ umount /dev/sdb1
  mike@linux-pc:~$ sudo fsck /dev/sdb1
  fsck from util-linux 2.34
  fsck.fat 4.1 (2017-01-24)
  There are differences between boot sector and its backup.
  This is mostly harmless. Differences: (offset:original/backup)
    65:01/00
  1) Copy original to backup
  2) Copy backup to original
  3) No action
  ? 3
  /dev/sdb1: 6 files, 23/1000176 clusters
  mike@linux-pc:~$ █
```

See that there are many
items of the "tmpfs"
type, but these are
merely temporary file
system storage facilities
in volatile memory.
Only the highlighted
items identify persistent
storage devices.

The **fsck** command uses
the same file system
checker that is used
during the boot process
prior to the mount
procedures – it should
not be used on mounted
devices.

Working with Accounts

User accounts are administered by the superuser. The **useradd** command will create a new user of a specified name, the **usermod** command can modify a specified user, and the **userdel** command can delete a specified user. A user's login password can be changed by the **passwd** command. The user's full name can be changed by the **chfn** command, and their default shell program can be changed by the **chsh** command. Each user may employ these to change their own details, or the superuser can change the user's details. The **pinky -l** command will show the details of any specified user:

Beware

Never change any aspect of the root user account. Also note that the options here for **usermod** and **pinky** are a lowercase L character.

172

1 Enter the command **sudo useradd tony** and your regular user password – to create a new user named "tony"

2 Next, enter the command **sudo usermod -l toni tony** to rename the user named "tony" to "toni", then enter the command **sudo passwd toni** and set a login password

3 Issue the command **sudo chfn toni** and enter the full name of this user, then issue the command **sudo chsh toni** and enter **/bin/bash** to set the **bash** program as the default

4 Enter the command **pinky -l toni** to see this user's details

Don't forget

The user's personal information details are typically more extensive than the brief details in this example – they are simplified here for brevity.

```
                              mike@linux-pc: ~                    –   ⌄   ⊗

   File   Edit   View   Search   Terminal   Help

mike@linux-pc:~$ sudo useradd tony
[sudo] password for mike:
mike@linux-pc:~$ sudo usermod -l toni tony
mike@linux-pc:~$ sudo passwd toni
Enter new UNIX password:
Retype new UNIX password:
passwd: password updated successfully
mike@linux-pc:~$ sudo chfn toni
Changing the user information for toni
Enter the new value, or press ENTER for the default
        Full Name []: Antonia Smith
mike@linux-pc:~$ sudo chsh toni
Changing the login shell for toni
Enter the new value, or press ENTER for the default
        Login Shell [/bin/sh]: /bin/bash
mike@linux-pc:~$ pinky -l toni
Login name: toni                 In real life:  Antonia Smith
Directory: /home/tony            Shell:  /bin/bash

mike@linux-pc:~$ ▌
```

A "group" is a set of user accounts whose rights can be modified simultaneously by the superuser. For example, a group may be granted permission to access a previously inaccessible file – all users who are members of that group are then allowed access.

Any user can discover which groups they belong to with the **groups** command and can specify a username as its argument to reveal the group membership of one particular user. The superuser can employ the **groupadd** command to specify the name of a new group, or **groupmod -n** to change the name of an existing group, or **groupdel** to delete a specified group. The superuser can also add a user to an existing group with the **usermod -G** command – stating the group name and username as its arguments:

5 Enter the command **groups toni** to discover that this user is only a member of a group named "tony" – added when the user account was created

6 Enter the command **sudo groupmod -n toni tony** to change the group name to match the modified username

7 Enter **sudo groupadd fund** to create a new group named "fund", then enter **sudo usermod -G fund toni** to make the user a member of the new group

8 Issue the command **groups toni** once more to see all groups of which this user is now a member

Hot tip

Group information is typically stored in a file at **/etc/group** that lists all group names, together with a comma-separated list of users belonging to each group.

173

```
                          mike@linux-pc: ~           –  ⌄  ⊗

 File   Edit  View  Search  Terminal  Help
mike@linux-pc:~$ groups toni
toni : tony
mike@linux-pc:~$ sudo groupmod -n toni tony
mike@linux-pc:~$ sudo groupadd fund
mike@linux-pc:~$ sudo usermod -G fund toni
mike@linux-pc:~$ groups toni
toni : toni fund
mike@linux-pc:~$ ▮
```

Setting Access Permissions

The **ls -l** long listing command reveals the access permissions of each item in the current directory as a string of 10 characters at the start of each line. The first is a **d** for a directory, or a dash for a file, followed by sequential Read (**r**), Write (**w**) and Execute (**x**) permissions for the owning User, Group, and Others. In the listing below, a script may be Read and Executed by everyone and the owner may also Write to it. The owner can both Read and Write a text note but others may only Read it. Three other text files may be Read or Written to only by their respective owners.

Notice that this user is a member of the group named "fund" that was created on page 173.

```
                      mike@linux-pc: ~/Docs          –  ⟲  ✕

 File   Edit   View   Search   Terminal   Help

 mike@linux-pc:~/Docs$ whoami
 mike
 mike@linux-pc:~/Docs$ ls -lt
 total 20
 -rwxr-xr-x 1 toni toni 34 Jul 26 07:49 toni-script
 -rw------- 1 andy andy 48 Jul 26 07:48 andy-notes
 -rw------- 1 dave dave 44 Jul 26 07:47 dave-notes
 -rw------- 1 mike fund 39 Jul 26 07:47 mike-notes
 -rw-r--r-- 1 toni toni 37 Jul 26 07:46 toni-notes
 mike@linux-pc:~/Docs$ cat toni-notes
 Here are Toni's notes to remember...
 mike@linux-pc:~/Docs$ cat dave-notes andy-notes \
 > mike-notes
 cat: dave-notes: Permission denied
 cat: andy-notes: Permission denied
 Here are Mike's thoughts of the day...
 mike@linux-pc:~/Docs$
```

Each set of permissions can also be described numerically where Read = 4, Write = 2, and Execute = 1. For instance, a value of 7 describes full permissions to Read, Write and Execute (4 + 2 + 1), 6 describes permissions to Read, Write (4 + 2), and so on.

See page 72 for more on access permissions.

Permissions can be changed at a shell prompt with the **chmod** command, stating the permission values and the file name as its arguments. For example, the command **chmod 777 myfile** sets full permissions for a file named "myfile". You must first assume root superuser status with the **sudo** command if you are not the owner. The **chgrp** command can be used to change the group membership of a file by stating a group name and the file name as its arguments. Similarly, the **chown** command can specify a username and the file name to change the user ownership.

1 Enter **chmod 644 mike-notes** to allow everyone to read this owned file, then enter **sudo chown mike andy-notes** to change ownership of that file – so this user can read it

2 Next, enter **sudo usermod -G fund dave**, to make the user "dave" a member of the group named "fund", then enter **sudo chgrp fund dave-notes** to change the file's group

3 Now, enter **sudo chmod 640 dave-notes**, to allow all members of the group to read this file, then enter **exit** to end the Terminal session

Do not fall into the habit of setting everything to permissions of 777 – use access permissions thoughtfully to maintain useful restrictions.

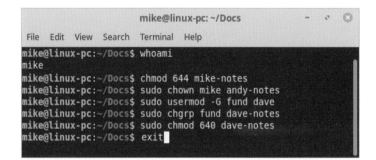

4 Open the Terminal to start a new session, then issue an **ls -l** command to see the changes, then read the files where access was previously denied

```
mike@linux-pc: ~/Docs
File   Edit   View   Search   Terminal   Help
mike@linux-pc:~/Docs$ ls -l
total 20
-rw-------  1 mike andy 48 Jul 26 07:48 andy-notes
-rw-r-----  1 dave fund 44 Jul 26 07:47 dave-notes
-rw-r--r--  1 mike fund 39 Jul 26 07:47 mike-notes
-rw-r--r--  1 toni toni 37 Jul 26 07:46 toni-notes
-rwxr-xr-x  1 toni toni 34 Jul 26 07:49 toni-script
mike@linux-pc:~/Docs$ cat dave-notes andy-notes
Here are some pearls of wisdom from Dave...
Here are acts of software derision from Andy...
mike@linux-pc:~/Docs$
```

Controlling Processes

A Linux system has many processes running at any given time, representing open apps, shell jobs, and background services. Each process has a unique PID (**P**rocess **ID**entity) number. You can see a list of every current process with the **ps -e** command – or those for a particular user – with **ps -u** followed by the username. The process owner can terminate a process by stating its PID number as the argument to a **kill** command:

 Open a **Terminal** window, then enter a command to begin a new process – for example, to start the **ftp** internet file transfer program

Enter the command **man ftp** to discover more about the ftp file transfer program.

```
mike@linux-pc: ~

File   Edit   View   Search   Terminal   Help

mike@linux-pc:~$ ftp speedtest.tele2.net
Connected to speedtest.tele2.net.
220 (vsFTPd 2.3.5)
Name (speedtest.tele2.net:mike): anonymous
331 Please specify the password.
Password:
230 Login successful.
Remote system type is UNIX.
Using binary mode to transfer files.
ftp>
```

 Next, open a second **Terminal** window, then enter the command **ps -e** to see a long list of all processes

Each PID is dynamically allocated by the operating system when a process is launched, to identify that particular process instance.

```
mike@linux-pc: ~

File   Edit   View   Search   Terminal   Help

mike@linux-pc:~$ ps -e
  PID TTY          TIME CMD
    1 ?        00:00:02 systemd
    2 ?        00:00:00 kthreadd
    4 ?        00:00:00 kworker/0:0H
    6 ?        00:00:00 mm_percpu_wq
    7 ?        00:00:00 ksoftirqd/0
    8 ?        00:00:05 rcu_sched
    9 ?        00:00:00 rcu_bh
   10 ?        00:00:00 migration/0
```

 Scroll down the list to find the Terminal windows listed as "pseudo terminals" named as **pts/0** and **pts/1**

4 Now, enter the command **ps -e | grep pts** to refine the list to just the processes running in each Terminal window

5 See that the first number against each listed process is its PID number – the **ftp** program is PID 2627 in this case

```
                    mike@linux-pc: ~           -  ℯ  ⊗
File   Edit   View   Search   Terminal   Help
mike@linux-pc:~$ ps -e | grep pts
 2619     /0     00:00:00 bash
 2627     /0     00:00:00 ftp
 2826     /1     00:00:00 bash
 3163     /1     00:00:00 ps
 3164     /1     00:00:00 grep
mike@linux-pc:~$ █
```

Highlighted here are the **ftp** program process PID and the message in the first window after you issue a **kill** command.

6 Enter the command **kill 2627** to terminate the **ftp** program process in the first window

```
                    mike@linux-pc: ~           -  ℯ  ⊗
File   Edit   View   Search   Terminal   Help
mike@linux-pc:~$ ftp speedtest.tele2.net
Connected to speedtest.tele2.net.
220 (vsFTPd 2.3.5)
Name (speedtest.tele2.net:mike): anonymous
331 Please specify the password.
Password:
230 Login successful.
Remote system type is UNIX.
Using binary mode to transfer files.
ftp> Terminated
mike@linux-pc:~$ █
```

7 Enter the command **ps -e | grep pts** once more to see the process is no longer in the list

Hot tip

At a prompt you can enter the **top** command to view the most active processes – press the **Q** key to quit.

```
                    mike@linux-pc: ~           -  ℯ  ⊗
File   Edit   View   Search   Terminal   Help
mike@linux-pc:~$ kill 2627
mike@linux-pc:~$ ps -e | grep pts
 2619     /0     00:00:00 bash
 2826     /1     00:00:00 bash
 3205     /1     00:00:00 ps
 3206     /1     00:00:00 grep
mike@linux-pc:~$
```

Exploring the Network

In much the same way that each house on a street has a unique address to which mail can be addressed for direct communication, every computer on a network has a unique number, known as its IP (**I**nternet **P**rotocol) address, which can be used to directly communicate with a particular computer.

You can discover the IP address of the computer behind a web address by stating the URL as the argument to the **host** command. In some cases, for large-scale websites, this may reveal multiple IP addresses:

Hot tip

Add a **-a** option to a **host** command to see all information about that host.

1 At a shell prompt, enter **host www.google.com** to discover the IP address for that URL

```
                    mike@linux-pc: ~              -    ⌐   ⊗
  File   Edit   View   Search   Terminal   Help
mike@linux-pc:~$ host www.google.com
www.google.com has address 216.58.209.4
www.google.com has IPv6 address 2a00:1450:4017:803::2004
mike@linux-pc:~$ █
```

The most basic test to see if another computer is reachable across the network sends tiny data packets to its IP address using the **ping** command. This continues sending test packets until you stop it, but you may limit the number of packets by adding a **-c** option stating the total number of packets to send:

Don't forget

The IP address used here is one of those for the Google URL – revealed by the **host** command in Step 1.

2 Enter the command **ping -c 3 216.58.209.4** to send three packets to this IP address – to see if it is reachable

```
                    mike@linux-pc: ~              -    ⌐   ⊗
  File   Edit   View   Search   Terminal   Help
mike@linux-pc:~$ ping -c 3 216.58.209.4
PING 216.58.209.4 (216.58.209.4) 56(84) bytes of data.
64 bytes from 216.58.209.4: icmp_seq=1 ttl=57 time=12.6 ms
64 bytes from 216.58.209.4: icmp_seq=2 ttl=57 time=13.7 ms
64 bytes from 216.58.209.4: icmp_seq=3 ttl=57 time=13.3 ms

--- 216.58.209.4 ping statistics ---
3 packets transmitted, 3 received, 0% packet loss, time 2003ms
rtt min/avg/max/mdev = 12.665/13.238/13.724/0.456 ms
mike@linux-pc:~$ █
```

...cont'd

In Linux you can discover the IP address of your own computer by issuing the **ifconfig** command to display the network interface configuration. If you know the connection device name, you can specify that as the argument to the **ifconfig** command to see an individual report. If your computer has multiple network connection devices, each one will be listed separately:

 Issue a plain **ifconfig** command to discover the network IP address of your computer

```
                              mike@linux-pc: ~              –   ×   ⊗
File  Edit  View  Search  Terminal  Help
mike@linux-pc:~$ ifconfig
enp3s0f2: flags=4099<UP,BROADCAST,MULTICAST>  mtu 1500
        ether 78:24:af:6d:3b:bd  txqueuelen 1000  (Ethernet)
        RX packets 0  bytes 0 (0.0 B)
        RX errors 0  dropped 0  overruns 0  frame 0
        TX packets 0  bytes 0 (0.0 B)
        TX errors 0  dropped 0 overruns 0  carrier 0  collisions 0

lo: flags=73<UP,LOOPBACK,RUNNING>  mtu 65536
        inet 127.0.0.1  netmask 255.0.0.0
        inet6 ::1  prefixlen 128  scopeid 0x10<host>
        loop  txqueuelen 1000  (Local Loopback)
        RX packets 3192  bytes 296885 (296.8 KB)
        RX errors 0  dropped 0  overruns 0  frame 0
        TX packets 3192  bytes 296885 (296.8 KB)
        TX errors 0  dropped 0 overruns 0  carrier 0  collisions 0

wlp2s0: flags=4163<UP,BROADCAST,RUNNING,MULTICAST>  mtu 1500
        inet 192.168.0.166  netmask 255.255.255.0  broadcast 192.168.0.255
        inet6 fe80::4426:1ac0:c500:43bb  prefixlen 64  scopeid 0x20<link>
        ether 54:27:1e:e9:ba:fb  txqueuelen 1000  (Ethernet)
        RX packets 26896  bytes 21006543 (21.0 MB)
        RX errors 0  dropped 0  overruns 0  frame 0
        TX packets 22548  bytes 4498695 (4.4 MB)
        TX errors 0  dropped 0 overruns 0  carrier 0  collisions 0

mike@linux-pc:~$ ▊
```

Hot tip

The "lo" loopback interface is useful for testing network applications locally before live deployment.

179

The computer in this example has a network connection through a wireless router, with an IP address of **192.168.0.166**, via a device named **wlp2s0**. Traditionally, the devices were named "eth0", "eth1", etc. for Ethernet devices and "wlan0", "wlan1", etc. for wireless devices, but a new naming scheme was introduced to overcome identification problems where multiple network interfaces are available on modern networks. The new naming scheme identifies the devices more specifically, to avoid confusion. With the connection above, the devices identified are Ethernet (**enp3s0f2**), localhost (**lo**), and wireless LAN (**wlp2s0**).

Beware

The **ifconfig** command only displays the status of active interfaces – add a **-a** option to include inactive interfaces.

Printing from the Shell

The **lpr** command takes a file name or path as its argument to establish a print job to send the specified file to the printer. Each job is placed in a queue awaiting transmission to the printer – when the job reaches the front of the queue, data from the file is sent to the printer and gets printed.

You can examine jobs in the print queue with the **lpq** command – each job is automatically assigned a job number. A job can be removed from the queue, before it gets sent to the printer, using the **lprm** command together with its job number:

 At a shell prompt, enter **lpr tux.png** to create a print job – to print an image file named "tux.png"

 Enter **lpr ballad.txt** to create another print job – to print the specified text file "ballad.txt"

 Issue an **lpq** command to see the current print queue

```
                          mike@linux-pc: ~/Data                    –    ✗   ⊗
  File   Edit   View   Search   Terminal   Help
mike@linux-pc:~/Data$ lpr tux.png
mike@linux-pc:~/Data$ lpr ballad.txt
mike@linux-pc:~/Data$ lpq
Samsung-M2020 is ready and printing
Rank     Owner    Job      File(s)                        Total Size
active   mike     1        tux.png                        57344 bytes
1st      mike     2        ballad.txt                     22528 bytes
mike@linux-pc:~/Data$ lprm 2
mike@linux-pc:~/Data$ █
```

The print queue reveals that the printer is actively printing job number 1 – the image file.

Before print job number 1 completes, issue the command **lprm 2** (or alternatively, the command **cancel 2**) to remove that job from the print queue

The printer removes that job while continuing to print the image file – the text file in job number 2 is not sent to the printer, so does not get printed.

Beware

A print job can only be removed from the print queue by its owner or the root superuser.

180

Printing from a shell prompt is not restricted to simply printing files – data can also be queued for printing using the **lpr** command together with the | pipe character:

 5 Enter **ls -l /etc | lpr** to print a list of the **/etc** directory – by piping results of an **ls** command to the **lpr** command

6 While the list is printing, issue an **lpq** command to see the print queue source is piped from standard input

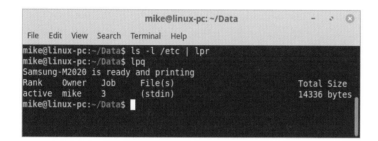

The ability to print in Linux is provided by the CUPS (**C**ommon **U**nix **P**rinting **S**ystem) facility. This provides a print spooler, which buffers data in a format the printer will understand, and a scheduler, which sends the buffered data to the printer when it is ready to be received.

The **lpstat** command has individual options to provide CUPS status information about the scheduler, spooler, and printer/s:

7 Issue the command **lpstat -t** option to see printer status

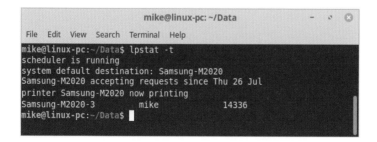

Hot tip

Where more than one printer is available, use **lpr -P** to nominate the printer to print the job.

Evaluating Expressions

The **expr** command enables you to perform simple math calculations at the shell prompt. It recognizes all the usual arithmetic operators, but those that have other meanings in the shell need to be prefixed by a backslash \ escape character. For instance, the * wildcard must be escaped for multiplication.

Each argument must be separated by whitespace, and parentheses can be used to establish operator precedence in longer expressions – but each parenthesis character must be escaped.

The **expr** command can also perform Boolean evaluations that return either true (1) or false (0) answers, and perform simple string manipulation with functions **length**, **substr**, and **index**.

The arithmetic operators are **+** add, **-** subtract, ***** multiply, **/** divide, and **%** modulo.

 At a shell prompt, enter **expr 7 + 3** to perform addition, and **expr 7 * 3** to perform multiplication

 Enter **expr 7 * \\(3 + 1 \\)** to evaluate a complex expression, and **expr 7 = 3** to make a Boolean equality evaluation

 Issue the command **expr length "Linux in easy steps"** to discover the length of the specified string

 Issue the command **expr substr "Linux in easy steps" 7 13** to extract a substring of the specified string

5 Issue the command **expr index "Linux in easy steps" "x"** to discover the position of the first "x" in the string

You can quickly launch a graphical calculator from a Terminal window using the **xcalc** command.

```
                        mike@linux-pc: ~

File  Edit  View  Search  Terminal  Help
mike@linux-pc:~$ expr 7 + 3
10
mike@linux-pc:~$ expr 7 \* \( 3 + 1 \)
28
mike@linux-pc:~$ expr 7 = 3
0
mike@linux-pc:~$ expr length "Linux in easy steps"
19
mike@linux-pc:~$ expr substr "Linux in easy steps" 7 13
in easy steps
mike@linux-pc:~$ expr index "Linux in easy steps" "x"
5
mike@linux-pc:~$
```

The result of an expression evaluation can be made to cause a particular action using an **if-then-else** statement. This has three separate parts that specify a test expression, the action to perform when the test is true, and the action to perform when it is false.

The **if** keyword begins the statement and is followed by the test expression enclosed within a pair of **[ ]** square brackets. Each part of the entire statement must be separated from the next by whitespace, to enable the shell to evaluate the expression.

The **then** keyword begins the second part of the statement, specifying the commands to execute when the test is true. Similarly, the **else** keyword begins the third part of the statement, specifying the commands to execute when the test is false. Finally, the **fi** keyword must be added to mark the end of the statement.

You must leave a space after the **if** keyword to avoid an error. Also leave a space after the **[** bracket and before the **]** bracket to avoid an error.

You may type the first part of the statement then hit **Return** to be prompted to enter the rest of the statement, or type the entire statement separating each part with a semicolon:

6 Type **if [`expr 7 % 2` = 0]** to test if the remainder of dividing seven by two is zero, then hit **Return**

7 At the statement prompt, enter **then echo "Even Number"**

8 Now, enter **else echo "Odd Number"**

9 Type **fi** then hit **Return** to perform the appropriate action

10 Make a similar test in a continuous statement by typing **if [`expr 8 % 2` = 0]; then echo Even; else echo Odd; fi**, then hit **Return** to perform the appropriate action

The backtick ` operators enclose **expr 7 % 2** so that operation gets performed before the test expression is evaluated – in this case, the remainder of 1 is substituted, making the expression **if [1 = 0]**.

```
mike@linux-pc: ~
File   Edit   View   Search   Terminal   Help
mike@linux-pc:~$ if [ `expr 7 % 2` = 0 ]
> then echo "Even Number"
> else echo "Odd Number"
> fi
Odd Number
mike@linux-pc:~$ if [ `expr 8 % 2` = 0 ]; then echo Even; else echo Odd; fi
Even
mike@linux-pc:~$ 
```

Scripting the Shell

Lengthy shell routines, like those on page 183, can be conveniently saved as a shell script for execution when required. Shell scripts are simply plain text files that begin their first line with **#!/bin/bash**, specifying the location of the **bash** program, and are typically given a **.sh** file extension.

Once a shell script file has its access permission set to "executable", it can be executed by specifying its path at a shell prompt – its name prefixed by ./ dot-slash characters if it is in the current directory.

A script might, perhaps, employ the **$RANDOM** shell variable that generates an integer from zero to 32,767 each time it is called. These are not truly random, however, as the same sequence is generated given the same starting point (seed) – in order to ensure different sequences, it is necessary to set it with different seeds.

One solution is to extract a dynamic value from the current time using the **date +%s** command to deliver the current number of seconds that have elapsed since **00:00:00 GMT January 1, 1970**. Using this to seed the **$RANDOM** variable gets better random number generation.

Arithmetic can be performed on shell variables, such as **$RANDOM**, by including the **let** command in a script:

Hot tip

Enter **RANDOM=1** then **echo $RANDOM** three times to see the pattern. Repeat both commands to see the pattern repeat.

Don't forget

Parentheses surround the expression to evaluate, but you must not introduce whitespace around the = character in the assignments.

1. Open any plain text editor and begin a new file with the line **#!/bin/bash**

2. On a new line, type a line to seed the **$RANDOM** variable
   `RANDOM=`date +%s``

3. Add a line to assign a value 1-20 to a variable
   `let NUM=( $RANDOM % 20 + 1 )`

4. On the next line, type an instruction to clear the window
   `clear`

5. Add these lines to output text for the user
   `echo "I have chosen a number between 1 and 20"`
   `echo "Can you guess what it is?"`

...cont'd

6 Now, add a line to read the user's guess into a variable
read GUESS

7 Type the following lines exactly to evaluate whether the user's guess matches the generated number and output an appropriate response for each incorrect attempt
while [$GUESS -ne $NUM]
do
       if [$GUESS -gt $NUM]
            then echo "No - try lower... "
            else echo "No - try higher... "
       fi
       read GUESS
done

8 Add a line to confirm a correct guess
echo "Yes the number is $NUM"

9 Save the script as **guess.sh** in the current directory

10 At a shell prompt, change the access permissions to make the script executable by its owner with this command
chmod 711 guess.sh

11 Enter **./guess.sh** to execute the script, then guess the number randomly selected by the script

Hot tip

The **while-do** statement is a loop that employs the **-ne** (not equal) comparison operator and a **-gt** (greater than) comparison operator. Other Bash shell comparison operators include **-eq** (equal) and **-lt** (less than).

Beware

Remember that the square bracket characters are operators – there must be space around them to avoid errors.

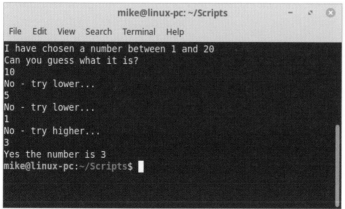

185

Summary

- The **sudo** command executes commands at a shell prompt as if a regular user is the root superuser.

- The Advanced Packaging Tool (APT) list of packages can be updated with **apt-get update**, packages installed with **apt-get install**, and removed with **apt-get remove**.

- Files can be compressed with **gzip**, **bzip2** or **zip**, and uncompressed with their companions **gunzip**, **bunzip2**, and **unzip**.

- File systems can be attached to the tree with **mount**, detached with **umount**, and checked with the **fsck** command.

- User accounts can be created and edited by the root superuser with the commands **useradd**, **userdel** and **usermod**.

- Login passwords can be changed with the **passwd** command, and personal details can be edited with the **chfn** command.

- The **groups** accounts can be created and edited by the superuser with **groupadd**, **groupdel** and **groupmod**.

- Access permissions can be modified using the **chmod** command, and ownership changed using **chown** and **chgrp**.

- Each process has a unique Process ID (PID), revealed by the **ps** command, and may be terminated by a **kill** command.

- The IP address of a URL can be discovered with the **host** command, and that of your own computer with **ifconfig**.

- Print jobs can be created with **lpr**, removed with **lprm**, listed with **lpq**, and status displayed with the **lpstat** command.

- Expressions can be evaluated with the **expr** command, and strings manipulated with **length**, **substr**, and **index** functions.

- Bash shell scripts begin with **#!/bin/bash** and are executed at a prompt by prefixing the file name by **./** dot-slash characters.

Index

M

N

O

P